EVERYTHING IN NIGERIA IS GOING TO KILL YOU

SELECTED ESSAYS

AYO SOGUNRO

Everything In Nigeria is Going to Kill You
Copyright © 2014 by Ayo Sogunro

ISBN: 978-978-943-268-4

Published in Nigeria by:
Shecrownlita Scribbles Limited
www.shecrownlitabooks.com
+2348064094006; info@shecrownlitabooks.com

"Gone Blogging, Back Soon" originally appeared on the blog "Akin" (www.akinblog.nl) as part of the Decade Blog series, January 10, 2014. "To Speak to an American Blonde about International Affairs, Press '1' Now" was originally published on *Bella Naija* (www.BellaNaija.com), November 20, 2013. Other pieces in this book have also appeared on the blog "Ayo Sogunro" (www.ayosogunro.com) at various times.

Production Coordinator:	Afolashade Lawal
Editing & Compilation:	Goke Gbadamosi
	Eghosa Imasuen
Book Design:	Jera Publishing, Georgia, US
Cover Image:	Ayomidotun Freeborn (Lucid Creative)
Author Photo:	Dami Agbotan-Kuku

This book is a Shecrownlita Scribbles Production

OTHER BOOKS BY AYO SOGUNRO

The Wonderful Life of Senator Boniface and other Sorry Tales

Death in the Dawn (a play)

Cracks in the Ivory Tower (co-authored with Goke Gbadamosi)

This one is for the cynics. For the:

"pestle-wielding critics, the unrelenting, self-appointed activists, the idle and idling, twittering, collective children of anger, the distracted crowd of Facebook addicts, the BBM-pinging soap opera gossips."

They care.

HERE ARE SOME IMPORTANT NAMES

Lots of folks have been instrumental to the ultimate existence of this book: some directly, some not quite so—but here are just a few of their names.

Some Names You Don't Need
My Dad: who runs a blog in his fifties, and has a perfect command of the English language.
My Mum: who has a perfect command of everything else.

Some Names You Don't Know
Afolashade Lawal: without whose love this book could have been published posthumously.
Goke Gbadamosi: with whose friendship this book would have been published posthumously.

Some Names You Need To Know
Funmi Iyanda, Lola Shoneyin, Obiageli Ezekwesili, Eyo Ekpo, Ayodele Olofintuade, Toni Kan, Bibi Bakare-Yusuf, Eghosa Imasuen, Bisi Alimi, Olumide Makanjuola, Michael Akanji: folks who have been quite generous to me with their advice, their time, and a lot more.

And Some Personal Names
Sally, Diana, Toyin, Enuma, Onome, Simbo, Vivian, Bisi, Temilade, Dayo, Yinka, Lawal, "Sagay", "Mr. Fred", and the incomparable "Mrs. O": folks who have been quite kind to me in more ways than can be specified here.

And The Most Important Name
Yours: for being confident enough to bet your money on this book.

CONTENTS

PREFACE

HERE'S TO A DOMESTIC AND PRIVATE END

"Reader, thou hast here an honest book; it doth at the outset forewarn thee that, in contriving the same, I have proposed to myself no other than a domestic and private end: I have had no consideration at all either to thy service or to my glory. My powers are not capable of any such design. I have dedicated it to the particular commodity of my kinsfolk and friends, so that, having lost me (which they must do shortly), they may therein recover some traits of my conditions and humours, and by that means preserve more whole, and more life-like, the knowledge they had of me."

—MICHEL DE MONTAIGNE, *Essays*

AN HONEST BOOK

The preceding quote from Montaigne probably sums up all you need to launch into this book. Consequently, you need not continue with this preface, for, as anyone who has read my last book will tell you, I am not to be trusted with a preface. Prefaces, which should be simple and unobtrusive statements of intention, usually manage to slip my grasp and emerge as recalcitrant pieces of prose demanding an independence of their own. And so, to avoid any possible misunderstanding, I now suggest—as usual—that you skip the next few pages and proceed to the first chapter of the book. However, considering that this book is a collection of essays, there is probably no point in skipping this preface which seems quite determined to become the first essay in this book.

Your logical reaction is therefore the question: why am I publishing my essays—has the public not suffered my troubles enough? This anxious question is even more relevant if you consider that most of the pieces in this book have been published severally on my personal blog, from where they have found their way to other places on the internet.

Well then, so what's my response?

A *proper* answer from me could state that this collection is a continuation of my personal quest for solutions to the socio-political travails of Nigeria; that this book represents my thoughts and commentary as a rising member of the church of social criticism.

But such a response would be quite untrue.

In fact, my motivations are far less grandiose, and much more self-serving: this book has resulted from the advice of friends and acquaintances who, upon their conviction that I was turning out to be a lazy novelist, advised me to pay more attention to my non-fiction. I took their advice and this book materialised, packaging into one volume the series of articles and essays that have subjected me to some fame, some infamy and a lot of indifference in the last four years.

I HAVE HAD NO CONSIDERATION TO YOUR SERVICE

In continuation of that thought, it becomes apparent that, despite the style and tone of my writing, this book doesn't exist primarily as a philosophical treatise on the trouble with Nigeria. Consequently, while a number of the essays here are focused on the Nigerian situation, many of them are descriptive in their intent, not prescriptive.

But this also highlights one trouble with Nigeria: the quest for quick and sharp answers to social problems. This is a reaction I get frequently from my Nigerian readers who, clearly exasperated with the angle of some of my essays, dismiss them as useless write-ups. When I wrote *Upon the Passing Away of Ayo Sogunro*, my daily routine was disturbed by dozens of phone calls and messages from folks who wanted to get reassurance that I was alive—or dead, maybe—because they failed to see the point of a literary eulogy. In fact, I received a fair amount of flak for irreverently writing my own eulogy.

I consider these reactions as one of the consequences of the embryonic nature of Nigerian literary appreciation and culture: a culture which has, over time, ranked the newspaper article over the fictional story, the academic textbook over poetry, and the motivational book over the novel. Few Nigerians are able to enjoy the use of words solely as an art; the majority expect any long aggregation of text to solve some practical problem, otherwise it is deemed to have no reading value. This is why, after I published *Why I am Corrupt* on my blog, an irate reader commented that I had offered no practical suggestions on how to solve the issue of corruption in Nigeria, but I had merely restated the puerile defences of Nigerians. I sympathise with such readers, but no: I am not offering quick fixes; at least, not intentionally.

Similarly, some of the comments I received on the satire against American conservative elements, *To Speak to an American Blonde*, (written in response to an Ann Coulter article ridiculing Nigerians) were from well-meaning folks who, confusing a satiric retort with a factual argument, tried to advise me on how to construct a "proper" rejoinder with facts and figures.

To avoid this type of frustration in reading this book, it is perhaps necessary for me to restate Montaigne that these essays are not meant to provide practical solutions to any problem or for any person. Instead, these are, hopefully, literary pieces; and their value is intrinsic, deriving from their own existence and independent of any external purpose. A painting is just a pattern of colours on a surface, until it evokes some emotional response in its viewer. I do not expect the words in this book to change the course of history or direct the affairs of men. If any of these pieces are able to make you sad or happy, laugh or cry, reflect or forget—then they have achieved their direct purpose as works of art, and any practical use is only secondary.

MY KINFOLK AND FRIENDS

A number of these essays are derived from, and have been encouraged by, interactions with a number of people on the internet too numerous to mention. These are, however, principally my blog readers and Twitter followers. I have managed a personal blog for a few years and had over 100,000 visits within that period. My appreciation of this social media activity is chronicled in: *Gone Blogging, Back Soon*. But while the internet never forgets, it is also a transient medium. Consequently, the internet only promotes the trending topic and consigns yesterday's news to the graveyard of forgotten links. If the internet were more intellectually inclined, links to classic literature would dominate the cyberspace while Ann Coulter articles would probably get a view or two. But the internet reflects humanity, and humanity lives in the sensational present.

This poor attention span of the internet presents two problems for internet writers. First, the internet judges our writings by their relevance to current events and accordingly we find ourselves being forced, more often than we would like, into the role of social commentators. Second, the great article one wrote last week would probably be forgotten as soon as this week comes around—one blog post is not enough to keep the author in circulation, no matter how profound.

Concerning the first problem, I confess that I am guilty of jumping into the fray without much prompting. As a lawyer, and a believer in human rights, the inclination to point out human and social abuses is quite strong, and it is quite convenient to be able to decry such injustice through my writings. I cannot therefore in good faith complain that the internet is too concerned with trending opinions and current events. Social media has provided a great platform for random commentary; the *Random Flashes* in this book are excerpts from my ambulatory thoughts on diverse issues, and—hopefully—they offer some compensation for those who want "realistic" solutions to their social ills.

The second problem, however, is more relevant to the evolution of this book. A book fixes the words of a writer in both space and time. The internet has moved beyond the time when some of these essays were first written, but a book grants them permanent relevance. This issue is also relevant in a socio-historical context: progressive societies forgive, but they do not forget; the less progressive society forgets, but it does not forgive. This book is a mild attempt to ensure that we do not forget, even if we forgive. In any case, my online admirers and my offline acquaintances—kinfolk and friends—would certainly not be saddened by the existence of this permanent compilation.

SOME TRAITS OF MY CONDITIONS AND HUMOURS

The five parts into which the book has been divided did not arise out of a deliberately themed collection of writings, instead they have been sorted out *a posteriori* and, maybe, tenuously so in some instances. Nevertheless, a casual glance at the preceding table of contents will give a general indication of my slant of thought and sleight of pen. A fair number of the pieces are directly derived from my personal experiences as a Nigerian living in Nigeria but with a universal frame of mind. The paradoxical lifestyle of the average Nigerian is the sum of this book: this is a lifestyle I have devoted much time to observing and also, actively participated in. My relentless pursuit of an understanding of the survival abilities of the average Nigerian in a system that is definitely dysfunctional is partly why, I suppose, the title essay of this book is the seemingly exaggerated and definitely dramatic *Everything in Nigeria is Going to Kill You.*

I have survived so far as a Nigerian, and so have a hundred million others. And so the social concerns voiced in this book do not indicate a personal desire to proffer solutions to social problems; instead, they are expressions of the coping mechanisms which seem to be built into the psyche of the average Nigerian. Some of us complain, some of us protest, some of us go spiritual and still many others go material, and also a few of us turn to the arts for solace—we write, not to cure other people of madness, but to avoid going mad ourselves.

My personal exploration of these lunacy-inducing situations in Nigeria and my private defences and personal counterattacks are the subject of the first part of this book. The second part of the book is a window into my private and public amusements at the foibles of the Nigerian society. In the third part of the book, I set free some of my rabble-rousing and barricade-mounting tendencies—quite unlike the fourth part, in which I climb on to more reasoned and properly educative arguments, hopefully. The fifth part of the book is a look at the politics of the Nigerian president under whose administration I have, so far, spent a fair amount of my adult life, and whom I consider as one of the parties significantly responsible for the seriousness of the title of this book.

More Whole, And More Life-Like

These pieces were written at different points within the last few years and would naturally reflect the mental and psychological states I had at those periods. My editors advised me to date them but I declined, principally to avoid the sort of chronological analysis that delights many a scholar. Nevertheless, I am inclined to believe that there is some philosophical consistency in the ideas bandied around the pages.

I have, of course, taken the liberty to revise some of the essays and, therefore, a number of them wear, in this volume, a look quite different from their original appearances. Not to be outdone, my editors have also thrashed a fair amount of my sentences as well. But these variations in detail are of little importance; the big picture is unchanged.

Ayo Sogunro
(Lagos, 2014)

PART ONE
METAPHYSICS
A Study of Existence

THE LAGOS BUS DRIVEN

First, the sweat—which gathering mass in the heat
Doubles up, proportional to the frequency of bus-stops.
Stopping? Pause. You curse. *"Driver! Move this thing."*
The syllables short and sharp. It's always inevitable,
This conflict of interest. The empty seats must be filled
But the filled seats must be moved. "DRIVER! MOVE!"
He heard: bus swerves. Left. Right. Left. *Tutuola's Drinkard*
No self-fault, but co-victim of renegade road contracts.
Oblivious, the conductor's grand symphony continues;
Names coalesced in swanky gutturals—*marijuanised.*
Your change. The mind warns. *Remember your change.*
More sweat: fatigue bristles with the sound of movement.
A slight rustle of the air. You inch forward. Grateful:
Direction is irrelevant as long as I'm progressing.
Then the bell tolls: alight with checks. Phone. Wallet.
Check.

1

Upon the Passing Away of Ayo Sogunro

A Eulogy

FRIENDS, IT IS A WARM and bright day today and we ought to take full advantage of this fair weather, therefore I will not bore you with a long speech.

Our late friend, Ayo Sogunro, whom we have come here to bury, is widely known for his repartee and witticisms, and he would frown to see us waste a day with winding speeches; useless to both the living and the dead. Nevertheless, we ought to do justice upon the passing of so great a person as he.

I am aware that a number of you here do not know Ayo Sogunro well, and have merely converged out of curiosity or by invitation. This ignorance is excusable; in fact, it is not your fault. That so remarkable a person like Ayo Sogunro should not be recognised by his society is the real tragedy of this funeral service.

What makes Ayo Sogunro a great man, you may wonder. Well, greatness does not consist of public accolade or tribute but is reflected in being aware of one's purpose—one's genius—and striving hard to achieve this in spite of all odds. Take time to review the history books and you will see that this idea, with or without public acknowledgment, is what has distinguished the life of great men. This greatness is in us all, if we allow it to grow.

Ayo Sogunro was such a great man, and the world would have marvelled at his genius if death had not cut his progress short at a young age. What was his genius? You may wonder again. What accomplishments had he attained? What technology had he invented? What lives had he improved, and what legacy survived him?

To answer your curiosity properly, permit me to trouble you with some of the history of the deceased. After hearing his history, you will be astonished that you have never heard of him before today, or that you thought him to be an ordinary citizen; and you will gladly celebrate him, as he deserves.

Ayo Sogunro was born in a little known hospital in a little known town. He was not privileged with a fancy hospital in Paddington or elsewhere, and his birth was utterly unremarkable. No newspapers announced the arrival of the baby, no social enthusiasm was generated and no public curiosity was stirred by the event. Right from the start, it seemed as if his society had conspired to make his existence a non-issue.

His parents were of ordinary stock, and they survived on their civil service salaries, raising a house with three children and several relatives, until his father lost his job and had to resort to ingenious businesses to keep the family from starving. Many of us are witnesses to the brutal economic history of the period. The lesson to be picked here is that Ayo Sogunro's childhood was no fairy tale fantasy. Let us therefore skip this part and proceed with our history.

Ayo grew up nevertheless, and attended a public secondary school at the commencement of the decline of these once respectable institutions. The classrooms had few functional windows, and fewer functional teachers; the students were more manual labourers than scholars. No sooner had his education begun than the school teachers went on strike for a full term. It seemed the Fates had a personal animosity towards the education of our young boy. In any case, the military government was not favourably disposed to teachers of any kind, and the educators were whipped back into classrooms.

With the lessons scarce and the textbooks scarcer, Ayo Sogunro's resourcefulness was put to full test, and like a hundred thousand boys and girls of his day, he managed to scale through public secondary school, somehow passing his WAEC, ill-taught and little educated. The fundamental essence of his entire education was confined to several topics in Mathematics and the English language, and scraps retained from other subjects. His proper knowledge came from dilapidated books in the even more dilapidated school library and the occasional private lessons grudgingly paid for from the insufficient household budget.

The travails of his public university days were even gorier. Ayo managed to secure himself an admission to study law, finishing in almost seven years a course meant for almost five. This was not due to laziness or failure. Instead, the civilian governments that had replaced the military treated lecturers no better than their predecessors and strikes became as fundamental to university education as matriculation numbers. Shall we talk about the quality of the education? Reading by candlelight in unlighted hostels? Making photocopies from textbooks or simply borrowing same? Juggling academics while "hustling" *via* small-scale businesses to support the meagre allowances from home? Let us not dwell on these unhappy thoughts.

Ayo grew to be a worker; earning a medium wage from a job he won solely by merit, without patronage or "connection". Despite his impecunious and unenviable background, he managed to achieve a good income and he paid his taxes and deposited sums for his pension. He never aspired for more than a fair opportunity to improve himself and contribute to his society. He sought no material riches and he did not covet his neighbours' property. Instead he sought to enlighten his peers, and he gained some notoriety for his criticisms of society, government and religion. His writings were fair and balanced; his admiration of life and humanity was unabashed.

We will never know with any certainty what really killed Ayo Sogunro. Was it the endless traffic he faced on the roads of Lagos, toiling to and from work to earn a living? Was it the headaches he suffered from the noise of the electricity generators that surrounded his accommodation? Did he suffer stress from having to seek bathing water every morning before heading to work? Could it have been anxiety over potential bomb attacks by terrorists? Was he in constant despair about the irresponsibility of the government? Sadly, a number of things could have been responsible for the death of this worthy individual.

But we can point fingers at the agents of his murder: the British who left a legacy of corruption; the independence leaders who strengthened the legacy of the British; the military dictators that raped the people they purported to emancipate; the civilians that succeeded the military without any obvious change in mentality; and, of course, the majority of the people, who happily allowed the atrocities of government to continue unchecked, either from having resigned themselves to apathetic acceptance, or misguid-edly trusting spiritual intervention to change the circumstances. They all contributed to the death of this fine fellow, as surely as an assassin pulling a trigger.

Everything in Nigeria is quite capable of killing any of its ordi-nary citizens. Ayo Sogunro is dead, and his country is poorer for it.

For as some of you may know, Ayo Sogunro was a man of letters, who aspired to great contributions to the arts. But the society he found himself in has little use for literature. A hungry man does not care about a finely crafted phrase. And so, Ayo wrote articles but was read only by a few; he engaged in public discourse, but he was little noted. This is not surprising, what hope does a literary-inclined person have in Nigeria?

Two profound examples of literary talent indicate that such ambitions ultimately end in futility: the internationally celebrated Achebe died in another country, virtually a stranger to Nigeria; Wole Soyinka, an internationally acclaimed intellectual, is still treated with disinterest by many of his own countrymen. Who then was Ayo Sogunro, this great unknown, to aspire to literary heights? We can only imagine the despair that must have suffused him at this pessimistic situation. Worse, this futility does not apply to litera-ture alone: in the social and physical sciences, in engineering, in philosophy, and in other disciplines that require abstract thought, Nigeria has successfully murdered its greatest prophets—and the little upstarts can be plucked off without trouble.

And so, today, we have come to bury Ayo Sogunro and all that he represents: the determined struggle to stay sane and productive in an insane environment. Here is a country where certificates are valued more than abilities, and where geographical origin is more regarded than personal merit. Here is an environment where the legislature makes crazy laws, a president's wife fights people publicly; and a dying president "governs" from a foreign hospital bed. The average American or European cannot comprehend this kind of environment, and the mental effort and discipline required to function as a proper person within it.

And here are the greatest accomplishments of Ayo Sogunro: developing an insightful mind despite the poverty in the educational sector; passionately producing his writings and opinions despite the expense of the telecommunications sector; stimulating and engaging with the written word in spite of the challenges of the literary world. In short, staying sane and productive despite the insane and unproductive governments of his day. Who knows what greater things he could have accomplished had he not been cut short? You are forgiven if you think Ayo's life was an ordinary one because he won no elections, led no destructive battles and stockpiled no millions of dollars. It is ignorance that leads a child to mistake herbal medicine for edible vegetables.

But, at least, today, we will sing of the great accomplishments of Ayo Sogunro. Let nobody deceive us that these accomplishments are not worthy of celebration. For in a country where every succeeding government contributes practically nothing to the improvement of each citizen, and in fact seems to actively repress any agenda for the progress of the people, it is remarkable that anyone can make anything of himself or herself at all.

The life of Ayo Sogunro reflects the best in us, Nigerians. His life shows our can-do attitude, our unwillingness to succumb to the rot, our ability to rise again and again in this Forest of a Thousand Daemons. Therefore, can we then stand fast and reject those vain parasites feeding fat on the rest of us—whether they are found in society, in the religious houses or in the government? Shall we stop making heroes of our own oppressors? Shall we not make heroes, instead, of ourselves? We, the everyday Nigerians, sane survivors in this uncontrolled jungle. May Ayo Sogunro rest in peace, and may his legacy rest in us.

Random Flashes:
ON SOCIAL INTELLIGENCE

*T*HERE'S NO FUNDAMENTAL DIFFERENCE IN *the mental composition of the "developed" societies and the African society. As a crude statistical example, out of ten people in a developed society, you will ordinarily have two geniuses or "above average intelligence" folks, six averagely intelligent people and two people of below average intelligence. Take your African society too, the same crude statistics apply, two Smart Alecs, six Average Joes and then two dullards.*

So what creates the glaring differences between the developed world and ours? The answer is probably simple: the first world has learnt, over centuries of misrule and carnage, that it is best to allow its geniuses to shape their society—from political ideology to arts and sciences. These clever folks lay down the blueprint—and the rest of society follow it to the letter. That willingness to allow the best thinkers draw up the plans for society to follow is what makes these societies the first world.

On the other side of the world, your average modern African society prefers to hang the two geniuses by the neck rather than listen to them. We choose who to listen to on the basis of age, wealth, tribe, family, "divine" appointment, entertainment value or some misguided sense of good luck. And that's why, in Nigeria, our professionals migrate to foreign countries; why we have chased away, jailed or killed off our thinkers, intellectuals, artists or anybody else capable of raising our society's intelligence quotient—while we adore the movie celebrities, hip-hop musicians, jet-buying pastors and inefficient politicians. We gave knowledge a well-aimed kick in the rear and gladly welcomed entertainment instead.

2

OF BOMBS AND THE LAGOSIAN

NOTHING ADEQUATELY PREPARES YOU FOR being a private citizen of a bomb-prone country. You don't wake up in the morning and check off a list to confirm that your security is adequate—not unless you're an airplane pilot, and maybe not even then. There is no transition period: one year you are a normal resident of a normal country with its share of normal violence—and the next year there is the serious possibility of a bomb being planted under your car.

In fact, you have to wonder if any mental preparation is possible in Nigeria, today. It seems that the sensitivity of the Nigerian public to destruction and death is declining in proportion to the increasing terrorism in the country.

So far, it seems as if the major Nigerian city—Lagos—had been spared from the reign of infantile terror. Consequently, economic and social activities have been, superficially speaking, unaffected by the security crisis riding the north of the country.

And so it was that, on my way to work on an early Tuesday morning, I found myself quite unprepared for what seemed, at the time, to be a confrontation with the maleficent forces that were running amok in the north-east of Nigeria.

That morning I had parked my car by a local intersection, opposite the University of Lagos while waiting for a colleague to join me in our daily commute. Along with another passenger I sat in the car as the local traffic converged; around us the suburban community nestling the University of Lagos came to life and diffused into the Lagos metropolis.

My other passenger was late, but the day was early enough to accommodate some delay. I flipped through radio channels and watched the road. Across from where I was parked, was a makeshift booth from which an official of the traffic agency—LASTMA—guided traffic through the intersection. From my side-mirror, I could see, behind me, the direction from which I expected my colleague to emerge. When the minutes lengthened and my patience trickled, I squinted at every appearing female figure in the mirror to ascertain if my expected company was close.

I performed this mirror gaze several times, alternating my attention between the road behind and the passenger beside. Shortly, a woman appeared in the mirror's view and approached the car. Just as she levelled with the rear of the vehicle she stooped, briefly, then straightened up and walked on past me. She was middle aged and unremarkably dressed. She didn't glance back after she passed but hurried on along.

I glanced at my passenger puzzlingly, but she seemed not to have noticed this external activity. Curious to see what had made the stranger pause by the car, I craned out of the window and saw nothing worrisome. I shrugged off my concerns and went back to the radio talk. The news discussed Malala and her visit to the President in sympathy to the cause for the rescue of the abducted girls. Bring back our girls, Malala also said. Fair enough.

Our colleague eventually arrived, and we were ready to continue the morning trip to work.

Suddenly, the traffic official was by my side—rapping the car window urgently and cautioning me to stop. I had not seen him come over. My engine was running and I had just started to turn into the road. Alarmed at the intrusion, I wound down the window.

"Is this for you?" the official said, holding up what appeared to be a laptop bag of typical size. It was a black leather bag and the texture looked rough and old.

"No. Not at all," I responded, slightly mystified.

"But I saw this bag under your car. I picked it up just now to avoid you crushing it."

"That's not mine." I said, while my brain struggled to make some sense from the emerging scenario.

"So who owns it?"

In the car, my two passengers were equally nonplussed. I gestured towards them for some confirmation that my brain was not missing a chunk of objective reality.

"No idea, officer. Thanks, but the bag's not mine." I said again.

"Who owns it?" The official repeated, expecting some sudden revelation from me. "Why was it under your car?"

Why was a bag under my car?

Some deep understanding of the security crisis in the country suddenly emerged in the morning air. Fresh attacks in Borno State had been in the news. Not long ago a major district in the federal capital, Abuja, had been targeted too. More recently, an explosion in the port area of Lagos had been claimed by *Boko Haram* as a bomb attack. The traffic official gently placed the bag down on the road and stepped back from the car. My passengers were now clearly alarmed but they kept mute and wide-eyed. I stammered out a response.

"A woman," I started. "A woman was beside the car earlier. She acted very strangely. Then walked away."

My right foot was on the brake pedal, and I felt a distinct quiver travel from my thighs to the base of the car. I switched off the car engine.

Why was a bag under my car?

All the while the officer and I kept on staring at the bag, awaiting some self-explanatory logic to a mystery that was verging on the dangerous.

"Where's this woman?" the traffic man asked.

I gestured helplessly: How could I know?

The official picked up the bag, and I tensed automatically.

"It feels heavy."

It feels heavy.

The sweat that gathered on my forehead was not just from the morning heat. I thought of stepping out of the car to get some air but, in the circumstances, that didn't seem a sensible proposition. On the other hand it didn't make much sense to sit in the car, waiting for *it* to happen. One could always jump out of the car and run fast—but what about my colleagues? What about the people around?

How much damage could be done here?

My knowledge of improvised explosive devices was limited: the black bag looked nothing like any of the crude contraptions I had seen in newspaper tragedy pictures—but it looked very much like anything that could have been concocted in a spy movie worth its salt.

The sweat that gathered on my forehead was definitely not just from the morning heat.

The traffic official looked worse than I felt. He had put an arm against the car—not leaning against the vehicle as much as preventing me from making a dash for it. He looked at me and his telepathic message was clear: *We are going to end this together.*

I thought fast.

"Call the police", I said. "Clear the area and call the police."

The official looked at me askance, and I realised he didn't know *what* police to call. He had no procedure for handling this situation. I shrugged; that was the best advice I could give. Vaguely, I remembered some public service announcement on handling suspicious circumstances. But it was a fragment of information, and the memory dissipated in the morning strain. I knew the official wouldn't be releasing me. Whether or not I had any knowledge of the bag, the business still looked very bad.

Seconds are ticking. I thought. *We stay here chatting and seconds are ticking.*

A bus called passengers for the morning commute.

The traffic moved freely despite the absence of the traffic official.

Life went on around us. People moved on. Lagos was unconcerned by our little spectacle.

Lagos, Nigeria is safe; we had been led to believe this. Lagos was impenetrable. The terrorists would not dare to invade Lagos. The impervious activity that surrounded us confirmed this idea.

Strange, but even within that nervous scene, I understood the irony of our joint helplessness: the helplessness of both the official and the citizen. There we were, acting out a potentially tragic drama as the city passed by, ignorant of the destruction that the morning could suddenly unleash. Nothing had prepared us for how to be citizens of a bomb-prone country. The representative of the law was just as powerless as I—both of us trapped in the inefficiencies of Nigerian politics and government. Security had been politicised; terrorism had been given to bureaucracy.

On that Tuesday morning, as we all lay transfixed on the Lagos road, playing host to the bag of doom, I realised again that we, Nigerians, were already socio-political victims even before we became physical victims.

But the danger passed: from afar a well-dressed young lady came running towards us excitedly. It was her laptop bag, she said. She forgot it at the bus stop and it must have slipped to the side of the road. Now she had returned to claim it.

The spell that had immobilised our little group was broken, and the traffic official admonished the newcomer.

"We nearly arrested this man," the official said with relief. "That was very careless of you."

He was back on familiar territory—the omniscient government official—reigning supreme over the bumbling citizen.

I repackaged my emotional state and restarted the car; the potential for danger had passed. But it could easily have been another newsworthy event in Nigeria's sorry tales. I drove off and joined the crowded traffic of workers on the Third Mainland Bridge, drove across the calm waters of the Lagos Lagoon, and the memory of the morning's drama regressed as the day took over.

3

Now That You Want to Marry

The Proposal

GETTING MARRIED, AS SOMEONE HAS pointed out, is easier than getting a driver's license. Consequently, a whole lot of people "get married" without much thought. However, the consequences of an accidental marriage are further-reaching to the individual than unsteady driving. When we say, "accidental marriage", as used in this paragraph, we mean that you have not sat down and thought out the factors we'll discuss below. You are probably only interested in marriage as the last stage of a romantic relationship—like a degree certificate. But marriage is more than just a destination, it is hard work. This article is not intended to scare or alarm you, but hopefully, to serve as a practical guide. Of course, life as a couple is better than being single, but a single person is far better than an unhappy couple. This guide is meant to help you become a happy couple or at worst, a happy single.

The Marriage

By itself, and even in the best of situations, a marriage is a problematic contract. It features the difficulties of having a business partner, an employee, and a boss all combined together in one transaction—often without any pay. Even worse, you cannot terminate an unfruitful partnership at will, sack the irresponsible employee on the spot or leave the cruel boss at a moment's notice without risking severe social, religious, and legal censure.

Naturally, marriage involves these social, religious and legal commitments not just to another individual, but also to that other person's lifestyle and life choices. It reduces your own individuality and it also limits your personal growth. You will become forced on numerous occasions to choose between investing in the marriage and investing in yourself. Whichever decision you make in such circumstances, something will definitely suffer.

All these considered as a whole, marriage is generally best avoided.

The Individual

Assuming, of course, that you have the will and inclination to enter into a marital contract, irrespective of the preceding cautionary paragraphs, then you have to be very particular about the person you intend to get married to. Ordinarily, without any marital involvement, this person should be someone you would eagerly hire, theoretically to fill the following positions in your life: business partner, consultant, guidance and counselling officer, career advisor, best friend, house help, handyperson, confidante, emergency number, loan agent, and personal physician—an endless list of practical requirements.

This individual you plan to marry will be someone whose presence you can tolerate at all times. The person is going to be in your face—night and day. Your personal space will be taken up by this person when you are not at work or outside. This other individual has to be a person with whom you are naturally in sync. You do not have to agree on every point, but you should understand each other well enough to resolve issues easily. Remember, you plan to make a lot of little and major decisions with this person for several decades. You will have to make decisions such as your wedding venue, names for the babies, a school for the children, the location of your apartment or house, the colour of your curtains, the style of your sofa, the décor of your bedroom, how you spend your income, your attendance of extended family events, your sexual habits and routine, your attendance at religious events, your level of interaction with the opposite sex, and a million other tiny little things.

Now pause and ask yourself: as a single person, are you currently comfortable making these decisions with this other individual? Are there current examples of such decisions that you have both made—that do not relate to getting married? Do you currently enjoy, and welcome, the invasion of your space by the person? Do you two "get" each other? Do you understand each other's psyche and motivations? Does this person know you well—or will the person be caught unawares by some facts about you after marriage? Can you vouch for the other person's actions or omissions without hesitation? Do you both agree on fundamental philosophies of life and spirituality? Do you give each other inner peace?

If you cannot give firm and positive answers to the questions above, then you have no business marrying this person. If there are still aspects of the person's character that irk or irritate you, then you should not marry the person. If you still intend to change that person's nature, then you are not ready to marry that person. Going ahead to marry the person under any of these uncertain circumstances is unfair to both you and the other individual. Just one issue out of sync can be the cause of a lot of future grief.

You love the person, you may say. But the fact that you love the person is not enough—a lot of girls love Justin Bieber too. And no, your love is not special. Everybody loves someone at one point or another. Do not confuse love with marriage—they are different things. It is possible to have a working marriage without the kind of romantic "love" you have in mind, and it is possible to be in awesome love and have a bad marriage. A good marriage is not grounded in emotions alone. Of course, it is good to have both features combined; in fact, it is best. But when it comes to a marriage contract, a practical and comfortable friendship with the person is much more important than an emotionally charged but uncertain relationship.

THE CIRCUMSTANCES

But what if you have met (and fallen in love with) the best person for you, are you *really* ready to marry the person? It is possible that you may be ready for the wedding, but totally unready for the marriage. The circumstances under which you undertake a contract of marriage are very important. You should be financially and materially prepared for the responsibilities involved in a marriage. You should have a fair idea of your income and that of your potential spouse as well as a potential idea of your household expenses. Marriage is not just an emotional commitment; it is also a financial commitment.

If the primary circumstances under which you have decided on a marriage are age or social factors, or from family or peer pressure, then you are doing it wrong. You should not allow pressure to force you into hasty decisions. You have to sit down and count the costs of life beyond the wedding. Remember, you are no longer earning and spending for yourself alone. You have to factor in the possibility of having a child within the next nine to ten months of the wedding. Are you able to handle all of the responsibilities involved? Is your potential spouse able to handle all of the required responsibilities? Only if you and the other person are practically ready, with measurable evidence of your readiness, should you venture into a marriage.

Random Flashes:
ON MARRIAGE

Marriage is one of those institutions whose rules humanity is yet to agree on. Different religions have different admonitions, different societies have different socio-cultural expectations, and different legal systems have different codes, yet most of these—especially cultures and religions—firmly believe their own stated rules are the most appropriate.

To confuse things even more thoroughly, different rules can exist even within the same religious, social and legal system! Thus, some rules allow a man to have more than one wife, others allow only one; others allow a woman to marry more than one man, to others polyandry is taboo; child marriage is allowed in some and detested in others; some rules allow divorce, others say no to it; some think the man's name must be the couple's name, others are indifferent about this; some are relaxed about children, others think children are the sole purpose of the relationship; some think the female should be subservient, others say the parties are equal.

This state of affairs, if nothing else, is enough evidence to point to the artificiality of marriage and give rise to some sympathy for humanity's continuing but pointless struggle to fashion marriage into a sustainable institution.

4

WHEN DEATH COMES KNOCKING

Philosophical Quagmires

WHEN YOUR DAD DIED MONTHS ago, and barely a week after we met, I acted sagacious. I delivered my one-liners and pithy comments instructing you, teacher-like, on how to face the future and how to focus on hope and not despair and more nonsense like that.

What did I know?

It's easy to be a philosopher when dealing with someone else's problems. Like a telescope sweeping over distant moons, our view of other people's problems is an evening's armchair adventure, the scope is narrower, and the distance is long. How profound! We wonder. How sad! We comment. How terrible! We console. And then we go off to sleep.

I confess I thought I had seen it all. Fathers have died aplenty. I've even contemplated the possibility of my father's sudden death for years, and I've become inured to the idea—I think. And so it was easy for me to calmly tell you that the worst had happened, that it was time to face the future; that every cloud has its silver lining and more nonsense like that.

I laugh now at the loftiness of my talk.

The puzzle of death is in its finality. Its finality, at least, for this world—I know of no other. *In this puzzle lies the ache, the sorrow, the bitterness, the fear*—ah, we fear what we do not understand. And in this puzzle lies the attraction for us, philosophers. Death is final. Let it go. We claim to understand death. Death is a timetable and one takes it when it comes, we say. Death is natural, we say. *A man dies, another is born. Nothing is good, nothing is bad, and life is merely a cycle.* I told you: the younger ones are there, your mother is alive, take care of them, and take care of her. I joked, and we concealed your tears in Abderian fellowship.

We laughed. It's easy to be a philosopher when dealing with someone else's problems.

You listened to me, your philosopher, and the sunshine returned to your smile, and you got used to the idea of future life without your father: no granddad for the kids, no father in law for the husband, no dad for you. But you got used to this, gradually and painfully. And we even began to joke about the man your father had been.

We joked. It's very easy to be a philosopher when dealing with someone else's problems.

Then today your mum died.

Barely eight months after, and death gleefully takes another swipe at your household. But Nature is not supposed to act that way! No! By all the laws of probability it should be someone else's turn! What more does Death want? You've paid your dues, for God's freaking sake! And God? Is there a reason for this? Oh, this is one of life's little events that unshakably point a finger to his nonchalance.

But I will calm down. I dare not lecture you now. What more do I tell you? Need we repeat the ritual so casually performed eight months ago? Should we go through the ceremony of healing again? How about the funeral? Are the same people who gathered eight months ago all present and counted? Wait, someone is missing: it's your mum. Is God playing games? Does his Grand Purpose depend on the double death? Or is his almightiness too busy watching over the birds of the sky and the flowers of field?

But I will be calm. Maybe there's no point in blaming God, maybe God is just the most convenient concept to pin tragedy on—to make sense out of the not sensible. Maybe this is just nature, after all. Maybe life is random and there's no purpose or order to things. Maybe death is not on a timetable and nothing has its time or date.

Maybe we simply die because the opportunity to die comes along.

So Death, personified as always, comes knocking without schedule or invitation. Maybe Death is strolling along the road, and seeing your house, he takes a fancy to the colour of the door, and so he walks up and knocks.

"Knock, knock, is anybody here ready to die?" Death says.

And just at that moment, you have the door opened, you're all dressed up and about to take a walk in the sunshine. And Death is grimly surprised, "Hello! How did you guess I was coming to the door?"

Random Flashes:
ON TRAGEDY

Christians, and many other non-Christians, don't shudder at the bloodletting in the Old Testament. The tragedies and deaths in verses and chapters seem far too remote for them to worry about the details. Instead they pick up the moral lesson to be learnt and continue on to the next story. Yet the singular death of Jesus is the theme of almost 27 books. A situation best explained by the words attributed to Stalin: "One death is a tragedy. A million deaths is just a statistic."

This is not just a Christian predilection. It's all too human. We ignore large numbers and focus on the smaller, manageable, ones. However the death of one man is just as tragic as the other—and you shouldn't fault a person's demise just because it was in the company of others. The Rwandan Genocide, the Jewish Holocaust, 9/11, The Nigerian Civil War, the Boko Haram war—we bunch up hundreds and thousands of individual deaths into one mouthable *phrase.*

But we go haywire over a singular tragic event: Anita Smith, age 24, a banker, single, was murdered while walking home from church.

5

DRIVING IN LAGOS AND OTHER CRIMES

THE OTHER DAY I PAID my annual contribution to the Nigerian Police Force: I invested in a Twenty Thousand Naira "Get Out of Jail Card", in penance for the heinous "crime" of making a wrong turn—described by the law as "overtaking another vehicle". I have no particular complaints about the financial loss to my pockets—I wasn't paying attention to the road or I would have noticed that I had missed my entrance. Also, the arresting officers were quite considerate: they gave me directions to the nearest ATM and patiently explained the practical aspects of the Theory of Relativity.

The lecture from the policemen was quite important, considering that my other option was a booking and a ticket, with the gloomy possibility of a One Hundred Thousand Naira fine. At the end of our interaction, I was not only happy to invest in the welfare of the families of the policemen, but I also tipped the gatekeepers with something extra as I drove out of the police compound with relief.

Yet, I still consider that I have not been treated fairly in the transaction: not because I had to part with some of my monthly salary, but because, in my estimation, my supposed offence did not justify the trouble I had to go through in atonement. There has to be an easier way to enforce traffic laws without disrupting the activities of citizens or handling the offender like a criminal. From the manner in which I was apprehended to the twenty minute drive to the police station—I didn't think I had done anything significant enough to cause the consequent commotion.

Here's the originating drama: I was driving to work, and trying to negotiate entry into a lane when, suddenly, armed policemen jumped out of a van and hastily surrounded my vehicle; transforming a benign Lagos highway into an impromptu war zone. For a brief second, I was bewildered—but my mentality was set straight when a scowling officer barked, somewhat gleefully, that I had committed a traffic offence under the laws of Lagos State. Naturally, I was happy to see the taxpayers' money at work, but I wasn't quite convinced that five policemen with assault rifles were necessary to take care of an honest carelessness. Anybody could have made that same mistake, I thought, and I tried to explain myself to the boys. But there was no listening air: my car was promptly commandeered and I was ordered to drive as directed. As I was somewhat in the wrong, and also had a healthy bias for my own continued existence, I respected their directives and headed in the opposite direction from my original destination.

And here is the problem: the average Nigerian policeman is still unable to distinguish between a criminal offence and a regulatory offence. Because every offence is treated as a crime, a breach of the most innocuous law results in almost the same level of official antagonism as a grave criminal offence. But crimes are a direct threat to the life, safety and property of humans, and so criminal laws are meant to act as rules of *human* conduct. Regulatory laws, on the other hand, are rules of *social* conduct, and would usually differ in various societies in their content and proportion. Someone needs to explain this to traffic law officials.

In a sane society, regulations are not enforced by guns and bullets—you do not need to commandeer a person's car for an expired driving license. Yet, in Nigeria, I have seen honest everyday people suffer loss of time and money for something as ordinary as an absent triangle caution sign. This is crazy. Why would the law be used to hamper people going about their lawful activities?

Of course, people must obey all regulations—serious or otherwise. Yet again, this is why the treatment of regulatory laws is different from criminal laws. For example, a policeman would have the discretion to waive a regulatory infraction, but he has no discretion to waive a crime. Still, discretion is a subjective element, and so human psychology is a vital part of police work: a policeman should know when to give a person a warning and when to book the person.

But, in Nigeria, the only psychology our policemen care about, probably, is their ability to gauge between the "big man" and the person who they can knock around with impunity.

To make a bad situation worse, the Nigerian society breeds lawmakers who misunderstand the nature of a crime: and so, in Lagos, for example, the offence of "overtaking another car" has a fine of One Hundred Thousand Naira. This is to force people to be self-regulatory, but how does the law compensate for simple mistakes of fact in daily commuting? It is one issue for a driver to deliberately rush past a red light: it is another for a driver caught in cross traffic at a junction to find himself inadvertently in breach of a red light.

Naturally, people will resist these rigid approaches to regulatory matters, which is why the scene of a car driver arguing passionately—or doing worse—with law enforcement is a familiar one on our roads. Consider a man driving along the road who sees a car on fire, he quickly pulls over and helps to douse the flames of the other vehicle using his fire extinguisher before proceeding on his way. But just ahead is a checkpoint, and, amongst other checks, he is asked to produce his extinguisher: he comes up with a depleted can—of course, nobody is going to listen to his story. He has the option of investing in a "Get Out of Jail Card" gracefully, or—depending on which law enforcement official is on ground—journeying to a station or the nearest bank.

It is the unlikely law enforcement officer in Lagos that will take time to consider the facts of the situation and decide whether to book the offender or issue a warning without exacting some payment from him.

And here's the irony of corruption: in a sane society, that same official can issue a warning and let you off without fuss. In our socially cannibalistic society, you have to pay the policeman to exercise a similar discretion. This is a discretion that exists morally, yet you have to pay for it to be exercised. Unless one has a strong point to prove—and plenty of time to see it through—a fair number of Lagosians would rather pony up the cash and continue with their hitherto honest journey.

The argument remains valid: the costs of evading the irrationalities of Nigerian law are far lower than the price of its application. The Lagos traffic law, for example, screws the average citizen: it has punishments but no protections. And so, would the average Lagosian really risk a trip to traffic court?

The injustice is worse when you consider that the makers of these laws are not bound by their own regulations: drivers of government and law enforcement vehicles are known to disregard traffic laws with impunity.

This is when you remember the Theory of Relativity and donate the requested amount.

Hence, you have corruption.

This is all unfortunate. Maybe all of this is just brisk business for the police: a way of redistributing the wealth. The government makes the laws, and secures its observance with heavy fines—trusting the policeman to know who to arrest and who to caution. But the average Nigerian policeman is not concerned with policy making, he simply spots the economic opportunities the legislation presents, and he bundles off the unfortunate traffic offender like a common thief.

I can hardly fault the policemen for taking care of themselves. Police work is tough anywhere in the world; but in Nigeria, it is damn near suicidal.

6

THE GREAT DRESS CODE DEBATE

A Thematic Scenario

(Office of the Head of Department, Dress Code Department. The HOD is seated at his desk, across from Ayo Sogunro, glowering at a sheaf of papers. After a brief silence, he raises his head and speaks.)

HOD: You're Ayo Sogunro, currently in your 400 level *(he pauses expecting a response and getting none)*. Will you answer me please?

Ayo Sogunro: Oh, I thought you were making a statement and not asking a question. In any case, you're right sir, that's my name and level.

HOD: *(Frowning)* Reports have reached my office that you consistently refuse to comply with the regulation dress code, and this is despite several warnings to you from the officers of this department.

Ayo Sogunro: That's correct sir.

HOD: And your defiance has, among other things, led to your dismissal from several classes by some lecturers thereby disturbing the said classes and distracting the lecturers, and that your conduct has encouraged students in lower levels to wear casual clothing and that, not least of all, you dared to wear non-regulation dress at official functions involving this faculty including a wake service for a former dean of the faculty where your informal dressing disturbed the uniformity of law students present and caused the faculty great embarrassment.

Ayo Sogunro: Why, I didn't realise I was so notorious.

HOD: Well as you know, this department was created to monitor student compliance with dress code regulations in the faculty, and anybody found wanting will have jeopardised their chances of being admitted to the Law School, or in extreme cases, have their admission terminated. But according to administrative requirements, before we impose disciplinary action, an affected student will be given a hearing before a decision is reached. In the paper before me, you have been charged with insubordination to faculty regulations and gross misconduct, and I am empowered to recommend you to face the Panel for Dress Code Enforcement. But I will give you the opportunity of stating to me why my department should not bring you before the panel. You may have your statement taken orally right away in a recorded session, or you may deliver it in writing within 24 hours. Which do you prefer?

Ayo Sogunro: I prefer to have it oral and have it done now.

HOD: Good, let's get it over and done with. Now, why do you refuse compliance with the dress code requirements, do you have an aversion for formal dressing?

Ayo Sogunro: No, I do not have an aversion for formal dressing; I just don't like the idea of wearing formal dress almost every day of my student life. But that is not the reason why I do not dress in the white and black dress code. I refuse the regulation dress because *the very nature of it is contrary to the study of law and in fact, other disciplines.* It is alright for lawyers who choose to *practice the law* in law courts to dress formally, but to restrict people who *study the law* to wearing a particular kind of dress on the basis that that restriction will enable them become good lawyers is not only absurd but cruel.

HOD: What, don't you want to be a good lawyer, is that cruel?

Ayo Sogunro: First, not everybody who studies law intends to practice it, some study law for the mere pleasure of it, others study it to be able to teach others, and more others study it with no idea what to do with it. I venture to say that less than half of those who study law eventually practice it, and even then, *fewer actually step into the law courts.* To impose a dress code on 100% law students because 50% to 20% of those students are going to be using it is clearly absurd. As for cruelty, I'm a believer in liberalism, and in this world. The study of any discipline requires the *freedom of the mind*, and the unshackling of thought; now *freedom of thought* and *censorship of expression* are concepts which do not go hand in hand. Students, mind you sir, I said *students* not lawyers, whose expression has been curtailed, will find it hard to free their minds. *The ultimate* *form of thought is action*, and where there is no possibility for action, there will be less need for thought. In fact, you will notice that it is students who comply most with the regulation dress that also comply the most with the lecturers' words—whether sensible or not, and ultimately, they become the kind of citizens who comply mindlessly with political irresponsibility without challenging them. This conformity is destructive to our country.

HOD: Stop there, young man. Are you so concerned with your unproved theories that you forget practical issues? One of the duties of the university is to turn out morally sound students. Will you have the future leaders of the country go around in leather mini-skirts and spaghetti tops?

Ayo Sogunro: Yes, if they are comfortable dressing in leather and spaghetti. You cannot force people to have a set pattern of behaviour when their own nature rebels against it. It is said that *'a person forced against his will is of the same opinion still'*. Applying this to university students; if we continue at this trend, at the end of the day what you will produce will be a lot of rogues in gentlemen's clothing—a factor which explains why despite centuries of "decent" formal dressing, lawyers are often in contempt and disregard in the western world.

But if you allow every student to dress according to their hearts' content, not only will you be allowing the natural freedom of expression, you also will be inevitably separating the wheat from the chaff. Students who are naturally inclined to a sense of decency which the law upholds will be noticed, and those who are not will be noticed as well. It will then be left for society to choose whose fashion sense it prefers to do business with at the end of the day. But where you force everybody to dress the same, you will be ultimately telling a lie to society to the effect that *"all these students are honest people, just see how they dress"* and that will be unfair to the general public.

And anyway, sir, without disrespect, you will notice that you said "miniskirts and spaghetti tops" a statement which clearly shows the direction of this whole dress code idea—that is, it is simply anti-female. I believe it is an embarrassment to us as intellectuals if, after our so-called enlightenment, we still see women as sex objects, because it is only a person who sees a woman as nothing but a sex tool that is drawn to the covering—or uncovering—of her skin. Such a retrogressive ideology defines the character of a woman by her ability to hide her sexual appeal—not whether she is kind, honest or responsible. A cultured person does not judge a woman's character by the dress she wears, nor is it the first thing he appreciates about her. The big point of promoting a sense of decency basically arises from the fact that some men just can't keep their hands off the direction of their eyes.

In an all-male school, few lecturers will be uncomfortable if all the students were to turn up in fitted jeans. But let a female student do the same and you will begin to see frowns of "noncompliance".

HOD: Are you insulting the lecturers of this faculty, the Law School heads, are you disregarding tradition?

Ayo Sogunro: I am sorry if I've said anything wrong, but if I'm right I can't be sorry. Any reasonable intellectual will see sense in what I have said; after all, the most compliant lecturers do not necessarily make the best teachers. I dare say the less sure of themselves some lecturers are, the more attention they give to the way they look in front of their students.

And anyway, I don't believe in being traditional, I only believe in being rational, if the tradition is reasonable, then of course I comply. That is not to say I am always rational, I only try to be. I practice a reasonable tradition—like wearing my wristwatch on my left hand. *(Laughs)*

HOD: Don't be funny. And anyway, you have not convinced me, I am sorry to say. That means you will have to face the panel, and from what I know, you stand little chance of escaping. By the way, isn't it easier to just wear the blasted white and black than be in this mess? What does it cost you?

Ayo Sogunro: Thanks for your concern sir, but I only wear white and black when reason dictates I do so, in other words when the regulation of the faculty coincides with my own rationale. I will not surrender my ideas merely because a panel thinks they are wrong. I have to get a sounder argument first and if I have to pay the price for my stubbornness, I will do so. Let me tell you of two great Americans, *Ralph Waldo Emerson* and *Henry David Thoreau*. When Thoreau was placed in prison for refusing to pay taxes, he was visited by Emerson, and Emerson said: "David, what are you doing in jail?" and Thoreau replied: "Ralph, what are you doing outside, when honest people are in jail for their ideals?"

HOD: In that case, this meeting is over, you can go, and await the letter summoning you before the panel.

THE END

7

GONE BLOGGING, BACK SOON
A Short Memoir

AS A UNIVERSITY STUDENT, I gained a reputation for being rather clever, and the satisfactory nature of this reputation encouraged me to develop an even more satisfactory habit of imparting some of my versatile knowledge to friends and colleagues in the form of tutorials—often unpaid for in cash or kind. In the course of time, I had gained a wider reputation as a fine teacher and I soon got used to hearing complimentary remarks such as: "You teach very well! You ought to become a lecturer, someday!"

Since humans are generally shaped by the expectations of society just as much as by their own personal choices, it wasn't long before the intention of being a university lecturer gradually settled in my thoughts as though I myself had originated the idea. Also, it was an easy ambition to aspire to: in those days, the qualifications required to be a university lecturer in Nigeria were fairly straightforward—all you had to do was complete a first degree and obtain a postgraduate degree.

As I was well on the way to finalising the first requirement, and the second being no more than one more year of the same, I was fairly confident that I would join the ranks of the academia quite soon after my graduation. I was so sure of this that I had already begun to stake out my own office among the staff rooms. I already had my class schedules figured out, my routine mapped mentally, and in keeping with my character as a young and naïve male—I could picture already the horde of admiring students of the feminine aspect. I was ready to be the archetypal Nigerian lecturer: lording it over enslaved students, with my word as law and my exam scores, final.

But the Nigerian Universities Commission was not so sympathetic to my career ambitions for, just before I left school, it became a requirement that university lecturers had to be possessed of a doctorate degree or have one in view. I was quite puzzled by this idea: the logical connection between the ability to educate students in the general aspects of a discipline and the possession of a certificate (for, ostensibly, having pursued a research thesis in a particular aspect of that discipline) was—and still is—lost on me. This decision was, to me, another step in the glorification of the certificate in a country where the possession of a degree was already more prized than the actual abilities of the degree holder. Even then, I knew a number of lecturers who bore plain "Mister" but were absolutely brilliant and even more lecturers that had the now required "Doctor" and who, as the man on the street would put it, "couldn't teach jack shit".

But my armchair protest at this unnecessary requirement was in vain. And with that came the dampening realisation that three to four more years of study would now be required before I was entitled to brandish my lecturing skills in an academic environment. It was quiet clear that the NUC had no urgent need for my services. It was also quite clear that I couldn't afford pursuing a doctorate degree right after school. In the end, I quietly pushed aside the ambitions to become a career teacher and took up a financially rewarding job instead, and without much ado, the ivory tower and I parted ways.

This experience is not unique to me. One of my dear mentors, a notable humanist and celebrated television presenter, once told me of her astonishment when the University of Lagos rejected her offer to give part time lectures to students. The complaint of the Unilag folks was that she had no postgraduate degree, and the fact that she had given similar lectures in European schools had no merit to the certificate-loving policymakers of that institution.

But along came the Internet and, for me, that has made all the difference.

You see, back in school, "browsing the Internet" was what you called the gruelling 30 minute stare at the eternally rotating Internet Explorer icon, anticipating the outcome of a dial-up connection that taught you the patience of the gods. Emails and rudimentary chats were the most interactive forms of Internet usage, "Facebook" was just a typographical error to be underlined in red by MS Word, and blogs—if they existed back then—might as well have been located on the moons of Jupiter.

But, as my professional life budded, and I became more aware of the other world that is the Internet proper, blogs gradually became A THING and soon, I found myself in possession of one. My first blog was a rudimentary package from Blogger that allowed me delusions of grandeur after seeing my name spread out on the Internet browser address bar. But with great grandeur comes great responsibility: blogging was work and I worked at it. The perseverance paid off. And before long, the readership trickled into the thousands and the lecturing ambitions of my younger years were transmuted into a stream of steady articles for my readers. The Internet is a school, and the blog has been my classroom—and I don't even have to perform the gruelling task of marking examination scripts. Of course, one comes across comments that make you want to take a stick to the reader, but even with those, the blogging experience is generally exciting.

I might go back to a classroom someday and rule over the students as originally planned, but for now, all the teaching I need to do—all over the world—can be done leisurely from my corner of the Internet.

With a click.

PART TWO
SATIRIC
Appreciating the Ridiculous

THE WORKSHOP FOR CONCRETE AGITATION

Join the workshop for concrete agitation
Help to dismantle the grand machination

A rhyme for our Oga, the legislator
Very well known for his tackling drill
They call him: *"The Tyson Senator"*
He bites his colleague as he goes for the kill
Eager to start the honourable fights
Always on behalf of the ruling side
He's a champion of allowance rights
And his house in Apo is our local pride
Today, he rides the town in big campaign
With stomach infrastructure and a merry face
We're happy to receive the imported grain
The *fila*, the *gele* and the expensive lace.
We can help his aims financially
But this time, no, not politically!

The people's workshop for concrete agitation
We decide which yarn is better for our nation

The President gave a speech last night
Desperate to show off his latest plans
How he was going to help our plight
And convert us to his number one fans.
We love our leader and his trademark hat
The goofy smile and that slow motion
He hasn't done much to get our pat
But his talk and puff deserve ovation
We were all eager to hear his yarn
And waited for "8" with a curious itch
But the electricity took flight at seven
Though we had a *Gen*, we missed the speech;
The President may have some important news
But our hard-got fuel was for better use

Come into the workshop for concrete agitation
Where the President takes a second position

8

THE ILIAD OF THE GREAT NIGERIAN POLITICIAN

AN OXYMORONIC IMPOSSIBILITY

WAIT, BEFORE YOU DISMISS THIS topic as an oxymoronic impossibility, try—difficult as it may seem when politicians are involved—to be open-minded. There are great Nigerian politicians—and they don't necessarily make the news headlines. Of course, I understand the fact that politics and politicians are not exactly the best sort of topics for intellectual discourse, and that the word "politics" awakens a mental image of the putrid; but then, this misconception exists only because the world is yet to study the ways of the Nigerian politician. Nigerians have perfected the art of politicking into a study worthy of intellectual interest. Now, let's discuss Nigerian political philosophy and how to be a great Nigerian politician.

THE WORLD CHANGES FOR YOU

Why would you want to be a politician, you may wonder, if you consider yourself a sane person at least? Even career politicians—and yes, that's a profession—rarely describe themselves in those words. In Nigeria, the accepted nomenclature include: elder statesmen, public servants, regional leaders, concerned citizens, or maybe even party chieftains; but never politicians. So why should you dump a comfortable professional or vocational career and risk your sanity or more in the literally cutthroat world of Nigerian politics? The answer is simple: divinity. The prime mover in Nigerian—and African—politics is a walking god. That's not an overstatement. And what human doesn't want a chance to feel godlike?

Let me elaborate: when you become a great Nigerian politician, the world changes for you; and this happens even before you hold office. Your words get news coverage no matter how inane, the most mediocre of your opinions are seriously analysed by pundits, and people who have never met you will kill, and if necessary, die for you. At events, you are the most respected personality: no matter how obnoxious you decide to be. You are the automatic speaker, the impromptu guest of honour, the definite chairperson. Think about this: The Chairperson. What will you not give to be the chairperson?

And if your ways are blessed with "divine favour" (as you will later call it), you get to hold a public office with: a salary of eight figures (or more), allocations and expense-paid trips, contractual opportunities—at best prices, a well-serviced bank account at home and abroad, a chieftaincy title, honorary doctorates and professor-ships, everyday congratulations for just blinking from people you've never heard of, a national award, a life pension, and if you die in office—a public burial. If you are really good at your game, you could get buildings and streets renamed in your honour, or maybe even a university or two; or the greatest of all honours—your very own face on the currency.

Good gods, who wouldn't want to be a Nigerian politician?

GENTLEMEN ARE NOT WANTED

What does it take to become a great Nigerian politician? How do you go about this arduous task? Not a few people have the definitely insane idea that the ideal politician is an honest, upright person whose delight is to oblige the people, and who places effective service before anything else. The impracticality of this idea is matched only by its baloney; and such fancies have no place in our democratic setting. If you attempt to follow this misguided ideal, your people you will disown you, label you as miserly and selfish, and frustrate you into an early grave.

Instead you should gather a reputation as a tout and a ruffian, someone capable of standing his own ground, a swindler with all appearance of a looter—then you can be sure of getting into office faster. You don't even have to pretend to be reasonable. Gentlemen are not wanted, and spiritually-inclined people are disallowed (except pastors).The intellectual people are not wanted. Career professionals (excluding lawyers) are not wanted. Economically successful businesspeople are not wanted. Writers, poets, artistes, sportspersons, scientists and innovators, Nobel Prize winners and their ilk are expressly forbidden. To be clear, these are not bad people, they are just bad politicians. A good Nigerian politician knows that he can hire them for use in the ministries and government departments as underpaid civil servants. But a great Nigerian politician knows how to ignore them totally. They may have the brains to excel in their fields, but they simply lack the brains to run for, and run a, public office.

But if you are an academic pretender, an "area father", a business failure, or if your business was built around some not-so-legal opportunities, or if you are a retired military man without any further ambition, or a former dictator, or a failing lawyer, you are exactly the kind of person needed in Nigerian politics. You were made to rule a country like Nigeria. Your past failures are the experience you need to captain this ship. You don't even have to be demonstrably Nigerian. If you doubt these assertions, look around and you will find evidence in almost every public office, with a few *accidental* exceptions—who will soon be rectified.

THE SAFE IDEOLOGY IS "NO IDEOLOGY"

The most important requirement for a politician is that he joins a political party. Any party will do. A few strategic points should be considered before making this relatively flexible decision: a ruling party seems convenient, but it is an association of individuals who are owed political favours for work done in the past, so it might take quite some time before you achieve internal relevance, or nomination for an office. However, a relatively new or unknown party would not carry you far, unless the party leader is a fiery challenger who is making waves, and whose deputy—by some incredible luck—gets assassinated, then you are sure to go places with a new party. But generally, what you need is a moderately successful party that has a foot in the door of power and where you can still shine personally. The party's ideology or philosophy—if it has one—does not matter. In fact, it is quite useless. No sensible political party sticks to an identifiable ideology, for in the long run, all parties will have to adapt to economic and social change. The safe ideology is "no ideology".

And, as surely as the snake sheds its skin, you should also have a capacity to change parties, easily and conveniently, without scruples. If you get into office through one party, you can cross-carpet to another: unschooled observers may call it cross-carpeting, but it is no more than a shortcut to relevance. In fact, it is ideal to get nominated and elected on the ticket of a small party, ramp up your nuisance value and then join the other, more important, party afterwards. Nothing personal, it's just politics.

GODFATHERS AND PLATFORMS

You need a godfather, and preferably one with a Mario Puzo predilection. This is for a simple reason: the godfather is feared by the people. And by "people", we mean the trade unions, labour unions, and other amorphous social and commercial associations that make up 70% of the voting public. These people will vote—consciously or not—according to the desires of the godfather. Be warned, however, when you assume office, do not forget your godfather—even if you change parties. Remember your obligations, and pay your dues to him. The scriptures are clear: the godfather giveth, and the godfather taketh away.

You must learn to make deals and swap promises. Never give something for nothing and if you can swing it, never give something for anything. Do not worry about leadership or service: if you can get some well-*liquidated* youths to cause a furore now and then, spray money at public parties, donate visibly to churches and mosques, then you have satisfied the expectations of the people. People expect nothing better from you, and in any case, no sensible Nigerian would believe your promises or expect you to fulfil them. The mass media is malleable, and the intellectuals and professionals will not bother you, at least, not until you get to power and, in that case, it would be too late for these eggheads to control you.

Look for a platform from which to launch your career. In Nigeria, things are so bad that it is very easy to succeed as a politician—traffic, bad roads, unstable electricity, non-existent water supply, insecurity, Niger Delta issues, terrorism, shaky education, unpaid minimum wages, excitable labour unions, recalcitrant fuel prices, payment of taxes, non-payment of taxes, missing pensions, greedy banking sector, currency devaluation, past military rule, potential military comeback, the presidency, the National Assembly, the judiciary, anything, and everything will do. Nigeria is a gold mine of opportunity for the eager statesman. Pick your topic, publicise your views in the media, stage a protest—or criticise a protest, kick some dust, express strong opinions at law events, at student events, at labour union events. If you are a militant type, organise a public palaver and then solve it: a garage fight, a religious riot, union strikes—commission some trouble and then be seen to put a stop to it.

Do all of these and you will certainly get elected.

AFTER YOUR ELECTION

After your election, the first thing you do: get a battery of lawyers.

A lawyer is a politician's best friend, to phrase it mildly. Do not be stingy with the law: and this rule will save your neck someday. Lawyers will handle your election petitions, sort out the allegations of non-qualification, dismiss the claims of corruption, and possibly frustrate the attempts at an impeachment. You can bet that these trials will come your way, not from the people you govern—they are not bothered—but from envious, less successful, fellow politicians.

Next, and this is even before you settle into the office, plan for your re-election. The road to re-election is paved with good appointments and strategic alliances. You must fulfil all obligations to party leaders and godfathers, accommodate their suggestions for appointees, award contracts to them at not-so-commercial prices, and pretend, good-naturedly, to be a loyalist. Now that you have the office, you don't need to show that you have it.

And finally—pay day. You have money, then spend it. Spend public money. Spend it as though money was going out of fashion. Here's a tip: prioritise recurrent expenditure, and spend only on capital expenditure that requires consistent maintenance and repairs. Generate contracts for your people to execute. A good government is a government of family and friends: insert your people—friends and relatives—in subtle, but key, positions and obstruct people who refused you support when you started out. Reward your friends and frustrate your enemies: this is the full meaning of justice.

And that is how you attain divinity.

The Great Nigerian Politician is, as Achebe describes, "A Man of the People". Reject the foregoing guidelines and you will begin to gain a reputation as, in Ibsen's words, "An Enemy of the People".

CAVEAT EMPTOR

On a worrisome note, remember that the people cannot always be trusted to be docile. You may push them around—but not too much. Otherwise, they will wake up, recover their senses and their dignity, and fight back. Then things will get ugly: unsponsored protests will rage in the streets, the mob will pull you out of your office and set fire to your mansions, the crowd will strip the clothes off your family, and the country will make you a spectacle and a laughing stock. So, avoid investing in any type of education—for if their minds are open, the fury of the people will be limitless. They will rise against you and put an end to your time.

But, really, every great Nigerian politician knows that this is a very unlikely scenario.

9

Why I Am Corrupt

NIGERIANS ARE CORRUPT, THEY SAY. I am a Nigerian and I know why I am corrupt.

I am corrupt because I am hungry. Because I need the food, the whole food and nothing but the food. Because I have to "hustle" if I want to see the food. Because without food I am useless, to myself and to society. A hungry man has no principles; morality is a luxury affordable to the well fed. I am corrupt because my hustle for food is filled with obstacles, because I cannot work as a labourer without tipping the foreman, because I cannot work in the civil service without greasing the wheels, because I cannot work in the private sector without "knowing" someone, because I cannot get a contract without contributing to the network. I am corrupt because I am hungry.

I am corrupt because nobody knows tomorrow. I am corrupt because my society has no welfare plan and the pension scheme is unreliable. Yet a portion of my salary has to go to the pension scheme, tax and whatever else the government decides. I have no confidence in the private sector—because the labour laws are unhelpful. Because my employer is able to fire me without compensation. And other people are waiting to take my place. Because my hard-built business may collapse any time. And it is a foolish person who forgets to plan for the future. I am corrupt because my daily bread is not secure. I am corrupt because I do not want to beg tomorrow. I am corrupt because I do not want my children to be corrupt.

I am corrupt because tertiary education is a status symbol. I am corrupt because academic achievements are required to attain a comfortable middle class life. And even though I have technical and vocational skills, I cannot get a job without a certificate. The right certificate can make a way where there seems to be no way. I am corrupt because I have to do whatever it takes to get the right certificate. Because I do not want to be condemned to a third-class economic life. I am corrupt because academic knowledge is power.

I am corrupt because I need a car. Because I need a power generator and a water pumping machine. Humanity has progressed and the individual must progress with it. And I want to enjoy the comforts that modern science and technology offer. I am corrupt because I would rather drive than walk kilometres. I am corrupt because our cars are treated with more value than our roads. I am corrupt because we have bad roads. And the bad roads have ruined my car. And I have to pay my mechanic to be able to continue the use of my car. I am corrupt because I *need* a new car. I am corrupt because God has invented the private jet.

I am corrupt because I am religious. Look, heaven helps those who help themselves. I have been taught this since I was five, that the race is not to the swift or the battle to the strong. Because my religion insists that I will prosper only through divine favour.

Because I have been assured that success does not come through hard work. Because I have *seen* people succeed in life without hard work. Because I must give my testimony too, someday. I am corrupt because I pay my tithes.

I am corrupt because the alternative is dangerous. In the final analysis, the price of honesty outweighs the consequences of corruption. Because there is no safety net for the honest person. Because a N100 note privately donated to the policeman is less cumbersome and less problematic than an honest trip to a Nigerian police station. I am corrupt because corruption is a logical process, because integrity is unreasonable. I am corrupt because corruption is ordinary: a mundane fact of life. I am corrupt because corruption works.

I am corrupt because the government is corrupt. And members of the government amass more power and gather more wealth. Worse, the lawmakers have legalised corruption and they simply allot public funds to themselves through the law. Yet, the economics of the country hasn't changed: the rich get richer and the poor get poorer. Because the government has an anti-corruption crusade but it has no welfare agenda. Because those who claim to tackle corruption belong to the corrupt system. I am corrupt because I don't trust the government.

I am corrupt because the system is corrupt. Because this country is a public limited company whose majority shares are held by looters. Because this is the Federal Republic of Nigeria Plc. where corruption is the price of a sizeable shareholding. Because honest people don't get to own a stake in the country. Because any Nigerian can become the president but a corrupt person stands a better chance. Because shares in the government are being traded by the insiders. I am corrupt because this is an unregulated stock market. I am corrupt because everyone else is corrupt.

I am corrupt because I want to stop corruption. I am corrupt because I am a social activist. I am corrupt because I cannot change the system from without. I have to join the system if I want to change the system. I have to win an election if I want to join the system. I have to join the party if I want to win an election. I am corrupt because I am anti-corruption.

But you are not a Nigerian; you cannot understand why I am corrupt.

Random Flashes:
ON FOOD

Any Nigerian (myself included) can give you, not just the problems of the country, but also a fair, if crude, idea of how these problems can be fixed. So why do we still have these problems around? Folks usually assume this is because the government has no clue on what it takes, and these nice folks are quite happy to educate the government on the way forward. But that's a wrong assumption. The government absolutely knows every in-your-face, down-and-out, expert-approved, consultant-sanctified, blueprinted, mapped out, long and short solution to the problems of the country. They know it far better than the average citizen can theorise. But they will not use this knowledge.

Why not?

Because the goal of every individual in government is to get the food, the whole food and nothing but the food. Engaging in constant cleptobiosis, much like an ant colony. This is a reflection of everyday life in Nigeria. Nigerian life continually revolves between the options of having immediate food to eat and risking a problem in future, or starving directly and fixing the problem immediately. The generally acceptable rule is to eat first and ponder later. Therefore, the government will only try to fix a problem that excludes the government from the pain of the fix—and too bad if the masses have to suffer that pain. On the other side of the battlefield, and especially in these days of Twitter and Google, the masses are beginning to understand this long con, and since they want to eat just as well as the government, they will also resist these kinds of one-sided fixes. Consequently, the country doesn't progress, and things remain the same. And that's what Fela calls "stalemate".

Naturally, the masses are not going to give up their hard-earned pleasures to please the government's "selfish" projects: fuel subsidy removal, import tariff on books, import tariff on automobiles. No one wants to suffer the fix to a problem while someone else gets away with the food. That's the real issue: not corruption, not insecurity, not the economy, not infrastructure, not health care, not education, not power, not agriculture, not oil and gas.

Of course, the ideal solution is for all of us, both government and governed, to endure the pain together. But, who wan suffer? The general consensus of the masses is: let the government stop its selfish spending and one-sided policy "fixes", and show a willingness to trim its bloated belly to a reasonable size, then the masses will be willing to share the pain. It's not necessarily the nicest ideology, but folks want to eat too.

So, your move, government.

1 0

THE IMPORTANCE OF BEING CORRUPT
A Proposal

THAT VEXATIOUS ISSUE

LIKE ANY PATRIOTIC NIGERIAN, I have once again turned my thoughts to the problem of tackling corruption in the country. Of course, better people than I have also expounded on this issue and given their own suggestions—none of which has worked so far. And because of this failure, Nigerians—and foreigners—have simply resigned themselves to fate, and accepted the continued existence of corruption in the country: like a tiresome but strong-muscled housewife—you can't stand her and you can't send her packing.

However, I am here with delightful news: having contemplated the problem again, I have thought of a way to eliminate corruption. In this regard, our religious readers have a point: only fasting and prayer could have done this, for it was after a long spell of impecuniosity-induced hunger that it struck me, forcefully, and with some physical bite, that the vocal social crusaders of my generation have been approaching the issue of corruption very wrongly.

Why do I think so? Because these current crusaders tackle the issue in the same manner as their ancestral adoxographers: writing long articles no government official will read, shouting on TV, demanding vigorous anti-corruption laws, crying for enforcement of anti-corruption laws, punishment of offenders, transparency in government—and a lot of other yawn inducing measures. Who needs all that *wahala*? Certainly not my hungry stomach. And definitely not our busy, hardworking governments. In any case, none of the suggested reforms has had any effect, even when implemented. In fact, the more one tries to enforce these reforms, the more corrupt the country becomes! As a general example, take the EFCC, which—forget it, you know how that hilarious experiment ended.

It is popular wisdom that only a mad man repeats the same process and keeps expecting a different result. It is therefore obvious that we cannot keep trying to tackle corruption the same way these social crusaders and activists keep on suggesting, and expect a different result. And if anyone argues otherwise, it is only proper to have him or her locked up in a mental asylum. Does this mean there is no end to corruption in Nigeria? Of course not! The solution I will propose in the next few paragraphs is foolproof enough to put an end to corruption in Nigeria—at least, as a problem, if not as a concept.

THE INEVITABILITY OF CORRUPTION
Now, it is generally accepted that although no sensible Nigerian praises corruption—not even privately—every sensible Nigerian, and his brother, practices it in one form or another. Trying to avoid

corruption in Nigeria is to prepare for an early grave. You will wake up every morning cursing the government, you will get delayed by policemen, your files will go missing in government ministries, your days will be spent ranting at civil servants, teachers, lecturers, clerks, gatemen, registrars, contractors, permanent secretaries, doctors, judges, lecturers, policemen, until you give in to a fatal heart attack, or at least, apoplexy. We will bury you with fanfare and continue with our corrupt lives.

What's worse: at judgment, you will be blamed for failing to "give unto Caesar what is Caesar's". The point is: we all have been involved in some corrupt transaction at one point or another in our journey as Nigerians. It's as much a part of life in Nigeria as soaking *garri* is in a boarding school. Nobody is proud of it, but nobody can deny it. And that brings us to my main point.

THE FINAL SOLUTION

You don't have to send a tiresome wife packing: embrace her and she will stop being a problem—assuming, of course, that she doesn't strangle you in the process. Treat corruption as a friend and not as an enemy, because fighting it only makes it stronger. So, we will no longer fight corruption: instead, we will make it our prime commodity. We will pass legislation making corruption a legal phenomenon. We will start by removing all those useless anti-corruption laws (since they are not enforced anyway), stop requesting transparency in government spending and activities, and start giving national honours to people who have demonstrated the most admirable cleverness in setting up excellent corruption schemes.

Now, before you throw your hands up in alarm, consider this. Nothing, really, will have to change. We are practicing all of my suggestions already, only that we do it secretly, instead of publicly.

So why suffer at both ends? Why not simply make the whole issue legitimate, and be done with? For those activists who keep predicting that corruption will destroy us: has it done so? No! In fact, corruption unites us all. The man from the North and the man from the South can jointly sit down together and loot everybody else. What better demonstration of unity can you get? Take a look at our major political party. As long as it was corrupt, it was a united house. Soon as some elements started pretending to an air of righteousness: breakdown! That's a lesson for us all: *corrupted we stand, pretended we fall.*

Of course, everybody cringes from the word "corruption". It does not sit well with our super-religious nature. You see, corruption is not our problem: the word "corruption" is the real problem. We have to fight this word very seriously. We will ban it from our languages, and issue a Nigerian edition of the English dictionary, erasing the word "corruption", and redefining those actions that the world calls "corruption" under names more suitable to our spiritual palate: "facilitation", "logistics", "miscellaneous", "appropriation" and so on and so forth. We will wipe out the word "corruption" from Nigeria.

Even though the advantages in a nationwide legitimisation of what is currently referred to as corrupt activity cannot be quantified, I will attempt to summarise some obvious benefits in the next paragraphs.

1. Conserving Public Funds

First, we will conserve the public funds currently spent on "anti-corruption". We all know this so called "fight against corruption" is a mockery, a joke, but we keep spending public funds on it anyway. This wasteful spending will stop. With our new ideology, we can cheerfully dismantle the EFCC, the ICPC and all those special fraud units of the police force. We will save: the money paid as salaries to the idle staff of the agencies; the expenses spent on importing technical equipment that do nothing; and the monies spent on investigations and prosecutions that yield no results! Do the math, and you will see the clear advantage in this.

Of course, there is the downside that governments in power will no longer be able to arrest political opponents on charges of corruption: but that can be remedied by setting up a Corruption Commission that would investigate and arrest people who have a clean balance sheet, but are opposed to the policies of the government.

Even more splendidly, we can stop wasting all the money we spend on elections, and simply allow the politicians to sort themselves out every four years—just as they have always done.

2. INCREASED PUBLIC REVENUE

Also, legitimising corruption will boost government revenue. Taxes can be imposed on income derived from corrupt—or rather, "miscellaneous"—activities. A number of Nigerians make more money illegitimately than they make legitimately, with the legitimisation of corruption, this excess income can be taxed as well. Our *Oga* Permanent Secretary no longer has to worry about keeping foreign bank accounts. The government will take its percentage, no questions asked. Here is the further usefulness of this idea: the money stolen—"appropriated"—from the government coffers is taxed again by the government! And so, instead of the money fleeing Nigeria to other countries, it can be utilised here in Nigeria, for the good of the general public. Somehow.

On a related note, the government can also factor corruption expenses into the national budget—so that we all know that even though N2oobn has been budgeted for education this year, only N1obn will actually be spent. As long as we all know this from the start it's not really an issue anymore, and the newspapers can learn to shut up.

3. CONTRIBUTING TO HUMAN KNOWLEDGE

Speaking of education: by legitimising corruption, we will open up a whole new field of human endeavour. Finally, Nigeria can take pride in its contribution to human philosophy and knowledge. We will strive for—and pride ourselves in—the title of Most Corrupt Country in the world. "419" will become a mark of honour. Our most corrupt politicians will be rewarded with even higher political offices. Our football clubs will demonstrate how to score 100 goals in a 90-minute game. Our school syllabus will include corruption-related subjects; the school awards will go to the students who can pass without even taking the exam. We will launch degrees in Corruption Studies, and encourage doctorates in Advance Fee Fraud. Nigeria will become a centre of learning, as people come from all over the world to hear our most corrupt lecturers share their inspirational success stories. We will be the Giant of Africa once again, and this time, for more valid reasons.

4. INCREASED FOREIGN INVESTMENT

We all love dollars and legitimising corruption will create an influx of even more dollars. This may seem doubtful at first look, but consider the possibilities. Shrewd businessmen will flock from all over the world to hide their assets in Nigeria, safe from the clutching fingers of their anti-corruption agencies. International corporations will prefer to do business in Nigeria for the free money they will get—therefore creating job opportunities for Nigerians. And when things go bad, we will readily grant asylum to international fugitives wanted on corruption-related charges, and even pardon our indigenous fugitives convicted in foreign courts. And, of course, we will swindle our foreign investors from time to time—as a matter of principle. And they will respect us for that.

ALL THOSE ACTIVISTS AND SOCIAL CRUSADERS

We will have to shut them up, firmly. In fact, I propose that we make anti-corruption a crime straightaway. Anybody found discussing how to fight corruption should be arrested and charged as an economic saboteur. No one really likes these people anyway—those impudent people, always demanding their rights and what have you; insisting on due process; criticising the government, preaching to their fellow citizens, refusing to bribe the policemen; and generally making life uncomfortable for everybody else around.

These people are selfish and ungrateful to the system that produced them. They simply want their voices to be heard and we don't need their hypocritical protests. In fact, hanging is too good for them. They should all be exiled from Nigeria, and sent to Europe and the US where their opinions are wanted.

Random Flashes:
ON HONESTY

It is generally agreed that the present Nigerian government is messed up.

The interesting part is this: a messed-up government is merely a composition of messed-up individuals who have emerged from a messed-up society. And so the people whom we elect into government publicly feed us with the same kind of deceit we like being served to us, in our own private lives. We are generally comfortable with deception—whether it manifests as government policy or spiritual authority.

We lie to others and other people lie to us. This socially acceptable deceit has made us all into public saints. And when it comes to morals, we are all fine religious folks. We abhor masturbation, reject foul language, condemn abortions, ban porn, criminalise homosexuality, censor Big Brother Africa shower scenes, strongly oppose nudity in the media, crucify pre-marital or extra-marital sex and lie through our teeth with a straight face.

Here's some unsolicited advice: instead of clinging stubbornly to a false spirituality, why not just embrace the reality of your sin? That ability to say "Yes, I did it" takes some guts, but it can go a long way to making your life more peaceful. Honesty is refreshing for the mind. You have no one to fear when you are an honest sinner; you have everyone to fear when you are a dishonest saint. And when we are done removing individual self-deceptions, then we can take a broom to a shitty government and clean it out properly.

THESE MODERN
CHRISTIANS SCARE ME

NOT YOUR GRANNY'S CHURCH

I WENT TO CHURCH LAST SUNDAY. This attendance is nothing special by itself; the south-western Nigerian society is as church-infested as a Vatican street. More than half of the Lagos population are consummate church-goers. Sundays, in the modernistic Lagos Island, still retain the medieval feature of being the day you put your best dress on. For many, it is the major social occasion for the week, a time to catch up with their social networks, enjoy the latest gossip, and send up a prayer to God for the downfall of the wicked boss in the coming week.

However, for a tough secular humanist like me, attending church in Lagos was a highly unusual event. I was literally dragged to the venue by a female friend (who also conned lunch out of me afterwards) amidst my protests of irreverence and sophisticated heathenism. The point, I told her plaintively, was that I could not honestly worship in an institution whose rituals I no longer had faith in. It would be, I protested, like an undergraduate attempting a sincere attendance at a nursery. I was way too sophisticated, I cried.

I forgot, however, that Christianity, unlike its main counterparts, is a constantly evolving religion, a continuously changing one—which is ironic, for a theology that, in general, disapproves of evolutionary theory. Christianity was started, a little over 2,000 years ago, by a band of roving fishermen in the hillsides of Judea whose rediscovered faith in their executed leader inspired them to profound acts of courage and missionary works. Their humility was touching, their message was simple: The Kingdom of God is here, repent.

So with the self-assurance only an unrepentant sinner can muster, I went to church and got a rude culture shock. The Modern Christians I falsely joined in worship floored my pretensions. Their sophistication surpassed my secularism, their worship more autolatry than idolatry. The church had moved beyond my ideas, and throughout the preaching, I felt as old-fashioned and out of place as a Buddhist monk in a shopping mall. By the end of the service, I had made up some helpful guides from my observations. These should help you on how to be a Modern Christian.

A BIBLE IS ONLY AS GOOD AS ITS PHYSICAL CONDITION. This is what I noticed—people had fancy bibles. You do not want to show up in church toting the worn-out family bible your grandfather was baptised with. Better to swing your empty hands into the sermon than drag along a weary script with half of Genesis in someone's trash and the books of Jude and Revelations hanging, literally, by a thread. Your bible should be clean and minty at all times. Leather-bound, gilded edges, with exotic commentaries and fancy footnotes. The pricier the better. Don't highlight the text, don't scrawl on the margins and don't fold the pages. Keep it locked up in a compartment in your car or handbag all week—until Sunday morning. Naturally, to aid in keeping it in its factory condition, your Modern pastor is going to make little or no reference to its contents in the course of the Sunday sermon. That's why you should keep up with CNN and Business Day while in church—there's more sermon material in there. Even better, use a software bible on a high-end device.

REMEMBER THE SUNDAY, TO KEEP IT HOLY: because, practically and theologically, all other days are ordinary and commonplace. You are granted Monday to Saturday to cheat, lie, backbite, quarrel, keep malice, fornicate, *swag*, party, swear, hiss, curse, get your groove on, ignore people, murder, assassinate characters; those six are days when you are meant to be vainglorious, impatient, arrogant, rude, cruel and generally get on with life. On six days you should labour, send e-mails, make calls, crack jokes, meet deadlines, set more goals, watch TV, read the papers, flirt, and basically get rich or die trying. But Sunday is truce-day: on Sunday you show respect to your creator by hitting the pause button on your carnal motivations and acting nice to the co-sinner next door. Monday is another day.

LOVE YOUR NEIGHBOUR—BUT NOT AS MUCH AS YOUR PASTOR: because brand identity transcends universal brotherhood. Modern Christianity is all about image laundering. A successful image needs a great brand. Choose your church, revere and emulate your pastor, and fight to maintain the integrity of your church's brand. A Modern church requires a classy and sophisticated brand with a logo designed by Alder and an ad campaign handled by DDB. The pastor must come with a brand identity and his pictures must reflect the values of the Modern church—wealth, prosperity, and luxury. God help the poor sinner who calls your pastor's name in vain. Remember, even if your pastor finds it difficult to say: "In the name of Jesus of Nazareth, rise up and walk", he should not be heard to say: "Silver and gold, I have not".

GO YE INTO THE WORLD AND BEAT THEM AT THEIR GAME. Actually, in the original bible script, Christians were to be a people apart from the world. But that concept is archaic; the world is a Christian (and Moslem—but the characters are the same) world, and since you cannot convert a land where everyone else is basically converted, the next best thing is to show the power of God in your life by being part of the Jet Set. You can reach more people and show them the way to your brand of Christianity by dressing in tailored suits and fancy gowns. It should be easier for a camel to pass through the eye of the needle than for a street beggar to enter your church and feel welcome. A failure to amass earthly riches is a sign that God is displeased. The more successful you are on earth, the more the people of the earth respect you—after all, you are the light of the world and the salt of the earth. How can you trudge around on foot? Even Jesus got a donkey at the end of his days; the least you can do is buy a fancy SUV. Preferably a Hummer—because you're just passing through this world.

BE COOL, TRENDY, HIP AND SMART: and flow with the latest Hollywood, Nollywood, Bollywood and other woody gossip and news. Feel free to drink (champagne and red/white wine), smoke (cigars), smooch around (occasionally), club (for business network-ing) and generally be the cool dude or babe on the red carpet. Be a social butterfly—an ice-cream boy, a *La Casera* girl. Say "shit", and "damn", and "fuck" when the occasion demands—but with exaggerated restraint. Just be a Christian, you don't have to be Christlike. You don't have to ask "what would Jesus do?" before every action—that's being stupid, not Christian. There is only one

Christ; you are just a Christian, anyway. Even better, God looks at the heart and he knows you love him. Even if you hate that bitch in the next cubicle.

CONCLUSION

So, people, those are a few points for you to digest, and I'm sure the Christian God approves my observations. If he doesn't, then three quarters of the Christians around have frightfully left the purported narrow path and are massing on Broad Street. But if you think these points are too tough for an average sinner to live by, I sympathise: these Modern Christians scare me too. But, remember, a Christlike life would lead you nowhere—on this earth.

Random Flashes:
ON RELIGION

And so what's the use of religion and spirituality? Religion is an internal influence, not an external one. Your religion is a personal spiritual business; it's not a physical force that will change physical circumstances for your benefit. Your religious beliefs will not change the laws of nature, logic and human psychology.

Whatever your religion—either the primordial ancestral worship or the more calculated notions of Christianity, Islam and their several counterparts—nature doesn't care. If you jump from a skyscraper and fall on a rock below, you will break something, whether you worship gods or not. Also, if you work studiously towards a goal, you will get it or get close enough.

Religion could give you knowledge, but it won't give you physical resources. Religion could give you enlightenment, but it won't give you personal progress. Religion could give you inspiration but it won't give you success.

You just have to do the damn work by yourself.

Random Flashes:
ON OLODUMARE

I like the Yoruba concept of God. It is possibly the religious interpretation of God closest to my idea of what (or whom) "God" is. The Yorubas call God "Olodumare" – a name that suggests unending possibilities of the being's essence. Olodumare, as noted by those who have studied the Yoruba cosmology, is the least mentioned and most worshipped force in the Yoruba religion.

You would think Olodumare would get pissed at this non-worship. But that dude is too cool to care. After all, humans are puny creatures he made in one of his more boring moments. So Olodumare relinquishes the rituals, worship, shrines, temples, and other religious humbug to the lesser deities to scramble for.

Olodumare doesn't need followers; he doesn't get angry, jealous, vengeful, worried or possess any other human emotional or physical attribute which the God of the major world religions are subjected to. And that's how a God should be: awesome and remote. Not a petty, meddling, egoistic, praise-seeking, interfering fellow.

1 2

How to Outwit a Blackout Economy

Note: One of the astonishing aspects about Nigerian life is the historical and present inability of the country to generate stable and continuous electric power supply. Astonishing to foreigners, that is; Nigerians have long learnt how to adjust to the blatant surrealism of modern life without electricity, and to help along with coping mechanisms, here are some not-so-well researched pro-tips on how to deal without "NEPA".

GIVE A DOG A GOOD NAME AND THEN GO AHEAD AND HANG IT: It's been years now since the federal government privatised and unbundled the irritating and frustrating National Electric Power Authority but you see, it doesn't matter whether you call it "Disco" or "NERC" or "PHCN", at the end of the day, the spirit of NEPA still inhabits the successor entities: NEPA's offspring are NEPA. I have observed people struggle to understand the Distribution Company concept or force themselves to mouth the cumbersome Power Holding Company of Nigeria—in the typical superstition that a name can make a difference in the personality of its bearer. The world doesn't work that way—otherwise a fair number of us will take the shortcut to wealth by a simple change of surname to "Gates". Likewise, the pretentious names borne by the new power entities won't generate electricity. Refer to a dog as a dog—and you can complain about it more effectively. More importantly, "NEPA" is pronounceable as a word and it makes good use of the lips and upper palate too. And so, here's the first rule in dealing with your electricity problem: don't buy into the "Disco" idea, be a stickler for tradition, recognise these "Discos" for what they are: old wine in a new skin, proudly continuing the legacy of **Never Expect Power Always**. So for the purpose of these tips, let's just give the dog the bad name as we proceed to hang it. We'll stick to "NEPA".

ELECTRICITY IS RELATIVE: Ask Einstein. If you don't know Einstein, ask your local nerd. You do not need electricity at all times. Really. Ask your local environmentalist. The value of a commodity is directly proportional to its scarcity—whether artificially induced or not. Like shipwrecked treasure on a desert island, electricity is useless when it is easily available. That is why Nigeria can survive without electricity. That is why *you* can survive without electricity—because too much of it becomes boring. NEPA understands this. You should understand this too. In fact, once you understand this point, you need not bother reading this piece further. You're fully qualified to write your own "how to survive NEPA" tips.

EVERY COUNTRY HAS ITS CROSS: If you are still reading this, then you are a die-hard, electricity addict. You deserve to be flayed at the stake of environmental conferences. Well, let's proceed then. When dealing with NEPA issues, a good way to come to terms with the problem is the acceptance of the tragic flaw that runs through the history of every country. A national tragic flaw, if properly handled, is capable of transforming a country into a great one. The struggle to overcome its procedural issues, to triumph over its administrative inefficiencies, to become the very best where it once used to whine and complain—these are the things that make a country unique. Read your history textbooks, and you will see that Nigeria is in good company when it comes to bad business. America had its slave trade, Britain had its colonialism, Russia had communism, South Africa had apartheid, and Nigeria has—lacks—electricity. You get the point.

BEING PESSIMISTIC DOES NOT SOLVE ANYTHING: I have often come across a strange attitude: people assume that an abusive or pessimistic outlook on an undesirable situation is capable of stimulating change in that situation. Like the irate parents of a wayward child, some folks consider insults to be the best medicine. Here's the typical scenario: you are on your way home after a long and tiring day, but as you approach the house you begin to curse NEPA, hoping that by some metaphysical or spiritual juxtapositions, your mental disapproval would propel the forces of electricity to connect your house to the grid instantly. And so you get home, but your house is in a blackout. The feeling of disappointment that arises in you is a warning against this inverse pessimism. NEPA is immune to correction and pessimism won't solve your problems. On the other hand, optimism doesn't solve anything either.

THERE WILL ALWAYS BE A BRIEF PERIOD WHERE ELECTRICITY WILL BE UNBEARABLY CONSISTENT: Maybe once in your lifetime, maybe twice, maybe even more. But as a Nigerian in Nigeria, you will experience this. There will be a time when NEPA's service will be so consistent it will make you rise up in anger. You will ponder and wonder before you enter the grip of indecisive activity. First, you will stay immobile; expecting the light to go off any minute, but it won't. One hour. Three hours. You will watch the clock in disbelief, agonisingly. Should you continue reading that interesting book—or should you get up and turn on the TV? But the light will not blink. Suddenly, you will realise the hours you have wasted, and you will jump up anxiously. You rush around performing the chores you need the available electricity for, and then ten hours later you will realise in astonishment that no, the power still hasn't blinked. Once again, you will discover your fridge's capacity to freeze, you will learn that your iron can actually burn clothes, and that your mobile phone's battery is not so bad after all. You will run out of movies to watch, and eBooks to read. And you will rage that TV stations should be shut down for poor entertainment value. This is the time when you will forsake the pleasure of your music player for ordinary gossip. And just that moment, that moment of time when you conclude that things are improving, and you raise your voice in blessing to the gods of electricity, the light will go off.

But that's normal. You've had your moment in the sun. The moral here is: you will experience it. Wait.

THERE WILL ALWAYS BE AN UNBEARABLY LONG PERIOD OF TOTAL BLACKOUT: This is a converse of the last tip. Every Nigerian expects an average of two to three hours of electricity daily. On a bad day, you may be rationed with an hour, or even thirty minutes. This is the norm, and of course, you have been groomed from childhood to cram as much activity as possible into those few moments of power. Nevertheless, no matter how tiny, it is power and it is *manageable*. But, brace yourself for that period in the year when, for three weeks or even up to six months—depending on your locale, you will not glimpse electricity of the variety dished by NEPA in your community. If you find yourself in this scenario, don't commit suicide. This is just a passing phase. It is a rite of passage, and we will all go through it.

YOU WILL BE TARGETED: At some given time, your house will be on the target list, NEPA's Blackout Book. This happens when you discover that everyone on your street, or in fact, your town, has light, but you are in darkness—for no apparent reason. Your bills are paid; you are connected to the same grid as the other folks; yet, you have no light. Nothing. Why? You ask yourself in the gloom of the night. You question your existence as you watch, from the darkness, the sparkling bulbs of the neighbourhood. Why me? Again, don't be frustrated. Today, your number has turned up. Tomorrow, it will be someone else's turn.

THERE'S ALWAYS AN ELECTRICIAN WHO CAN FIX THE TENSION WIRE: So why are you worried about the fact that your line has been disconnected?

DON'T BURY YOUR HEAD IN THE SAND: There is no light. That's the plain ugly truth. Nigerians are a resilient lot—and sometimes they confuse their own adaptations for reality. You probably spend a great deal of your day at the workplace, in front of a computer, possibly enjoying the serenity of a corporate environment. Your work is uninterrupted by a power failure. The AC units are wonderful, and life is good. But don't kid yourself. That is not reality: what you see is the handiwork of electricity generators and power inverters doing their work nicely. Look, let's put it this way: *there is no light.* Don't let the fantasy of generator plants deceive you. Look everywhere: office skyscrapers, affluent residential estates, five-star hotels, private mansions, it doesn't matter. There is no light, no light at all. You may not know the costs of this false electric power, but ask the person who pays the diesel bills: he is cursing madly, somewhere.

If all else fails, try the coal iron: Ignoring electricity is the best revenge against NEPA. When you go back to the basics, you will discover a whole new world of substitutes for your electricity problems. Take ironing, for example. Not everyone has a powerful generator that can power these small monsters. But if you allow the frustrations of NEPA to get to you, and you desperately wear your wrinkled attire to work, on the same day a European delegation is visiting the office to finalise a contract—

Anyway, just try the coal iron—it really works.

13

THE JOYS OF UNFRIENDING
An Antisocial Guide to Social Media

"I love mankind, it's people I can't stand."
—CHARLES M. SCHULZ

LOGIN

ARE YOU TIRED OF TODAY'S overhyping of a socially connected life? Do you look at your Facebook account and wonder how you accumulated so many "friends"? Are you convinced that there is a disconnect between the facts of your real life (consisting of a few friends and several acquaintances) and your social media relationships (consisting of a thousand friends)? Have you been in despair since you wasted time watching *The Social Network* and have since been seeking revenge? Then you need to partake from the elixir of "Unfriending". In this short piece, I may not be able to address all your social network concerns (a therapist is highly recommended for that), but I will guide you to the joys of Unfriending.

Of course, Facebook is a great place to start a business network and monitor your failed and fantasy romantic interests, but it's also an easy place to clutter up your emotionally stressed life with additional emotional garbage—disguised as "Facebook friends". Well, just as you regularly clear out your wardrobe and irregularly clean the house, you should find time to clean-up your Facebook account. As a general rule, I recommend a clean-up exercise once every three months. Some people already do this. However, the problem with most approaches to Unfriending is this: a number of people weed out "friends" in a haphazard manner and inadvertently turn a healthy exercise into a doubt-filled, profile double-checking cyber nightmare. If you are ready to tackle the unneeded friends in your life, and spend more quality time on Facebook—like you used to years ago—the following paragraphs will guide your social defenestration in a way that maintains your perspective and turns Unfriending into a fun activity.

THE GHOST FRIENDS

Our first set of so-called friends shouldn't take a lot of time to clear out of the way. Just do a quick scan of your Facebook friends. Anyone whose face or name you spend more than 5 seconds trying to recollect is not worthy of your friendship—and you are not worthy of theirs. You have to kick hopeful possibility and nostalgic feeling out of the way, and get honest with yourself. These relationships are floppier than a diskette and about as useful as Betamax. You could sit with these "friends" in a bus and still not recognise them anymore than you would recognise a piece of moon rock at a stone quarry. You don't give a care in the world about the person and you know it. Just press the Unfriend button. Even if you recollect the name or face in five minutes, it's too late. In our hypothetical bus, five minutes is far too late to get a feeling of familiarity—the person would probably have got off the bus anyway. Save yourself from the embarrassment of a re-introduction, you're probably also not memorable to the person.

The Business Card Friends

Back in the pre-Facebook days, when you met some vaguely promising person at a party or business meeting, you exchanged business cards and promised to call sometime soon. Promptly, soon as you got home, you tossed the card into a box to join a growing heap of similar stationery and you forgot about the person. You don't feel bad about the card tossing, because the other party has certainly done the same to your card. Life goes on and you live happily ever after until you bump into the person again and repeat the process—and you both apologise for somehow losing each other's cards.

In this age of social media, the antics are similar. After a party or a meeting, you both cheerfully give out your Facebook names or—in a moment of alcoholic camaraderie—maybe even add each other on the spot. And then you promptly forget each other's existence. Meanwhile your "friend" list gets swollen by another joker you don't care about. These "one-off" people are the next group you have to Unfriend. Unlike the Ghost Friends, you do recollect who these people are, except that you've had no further dealings with them since you first met. In plain language: you don't need each other. Don't be fooled by motivational axioms that preach the importance of everyone. Not everyone is important to you. Your random meeting with a stranger at a party was neither destined, nor will it ever amount to being the next Great Friendship. As a matter of fact, you've probably not even messaged each other since the famous party. So, be honest and say goodbye to your hasty promise of eternal poking and tagging: unfriend that clown.

THE MEMORY CIRCUIT FRIENDS

This is the category for all the people you knew from childhood, primary school, high school, college, university and, if you're old enough, previous work. This is the drag-along and tag-along crew whose sole connection with your current life is the shared past. These people insist on burdening your memory with "the good old days" and "back in those days" chat messages. They start their messages to you by launching a time capsule: "Hello, I was in school with you, I used to sit by the window" (Roll your eyes appropriately); "Remember Jane? She's now married with two kids!" (Roll your eyes some more); "Do you remember Mr. John the Economics teacher? He died last year!" (Just keep rolling it). You can't even recall some of these folks or circumstances they keep referencing. And those facts are people you remember are too remote to be of any use to your life. These "friends" only make your Facebook feed even more irritating. Besides, you don't need the bad memories, start up with the Unfriending button and get on with the pruning. Of course, if you've made it to the top of your world (unlikely) and you have more than enough wealth to boast about (even more unlikely), and you are able to handle a show of peer envy (very likely), then instead of Unfriending them, turn the tables round and get them to Unfriend you by reminding them constantly, and in the most obnoxious way possible, how you've made it in life and how your current life is so far better than whatever you both shared in the faraway past.

THE MISCELLANEOUS ANNOYING FRIENDS

When you've cleared out the characters in the previous categories, you should have enough breathing room to spread out a football field. However, if your surplus is still more than your deletions and you still feel a bit choked up, there are a few more categories of people I have tagged as miscellaneous—considering that the degree of their uselessness is subjective, varying according to your ability to tolerate unsolicited bullshit. First, the "**Non-Users**": these are the friends that set up an account five years ago and still don't have a profile picture or a status update. They think being "on Facebook" is all about registering an account—while maintaining a strictly offline interaction with you, please put them out of their misery and Unfriend them speedily. Second, consider removing the "**Juvenilely Named**": people who think of the most insufferable way to disguise their names—so you get John as "Jawn" and Jane as "Jhayne"–and you login one morning to see that one Jawn "Jhayne" ThawMoss is somehow your friend: Unfriend the spelling hell out of him. Third, the "**Unfriendly Friends**": these are the people you hate in reality but are still your "friends' on Facebook, just so you can maintain the illusion of goodwill. It's bad enough that you can't stand them in flesh, why suffer their online presence? Fourth, are the "**Relationship Unpotentials**": those people you added only because you saw that they were single and who are now "in a relationship"—well, what are you still waiting for, a marriage?

LOGOUT

Keeping in sync with Sod's Law, some "friends" that you haven't interacted with in three years will send you an angry message the next day after you Unfriend them. Don't get rattled or apologetic. Just explain calmly that you were trying out some new Unfriending Software that automatically zaps off people who don't meet certain criteria, and then this terrible software went ahead and deleted your best buddies. You know how software is, right? Once placated, add any such meddlesome interlopers as friends again—and then release the Unfriending Software to do its work, in another three months.

14

TO SPEAK TO AN AMERICAN BLONDE ABOUT INTERNATIONAL AFFAIRS, PRESS '1

A Satire

Note: *In typical conservative fashion, American public speaker, Ann Coulter derided the Obamacare website sometime in 2013—which is none of our business, except that she insulted all of Nigerian society while at it. Of course, helpful criticisms from foreign observers are welcome, but direct insults require a satirical rejoinder.*

I N A COMICAL CONFLUENCE OF America's two most fundamental issues—freedom of expression and insane tolerance of
idle celebrities—we, Nigerians, found out that a significant
commentator on critical social issues on behalf of hundreds of
thousands of American citizens is a woman idiomatically regarded
as "a dumb blonde".

Nigerians already know that a number of American celebrity blondes have been exposed as lacking vital components of human knowledge, therefore limiting them to entertainment value only. However, we are now dumbfounded that these uninformed celebrities also comment on vital issues of American public policy. Nigerians, and citizens of other countries, would be eternally grateful if the American Department of Health and Human Services, and indeed, the entire American public, screen out these 19th-century-themed commentators with a good, old-fashioned "STFU" before allowing them to broadcast their opinions to the world. (But rest assured: if a country's national dignity is eroded as a result of these abnormal commentaries, no one will be more upset about it than the American public.)

It's a blessing to America, after all, that the conservative sector ratings have crashed even more than the Obamacare website any time these uninformed commentaries are broadcast to the public.

Of course, celebrity political commentators are drawn from failed politicians, unreadable authors, attention-seeking columnists and front-persons for the Republican National Committee.

In fact, call right up and request advice on public issues touching on international affairs from any one of these folks! What could go wrong?

If you call today, you can book Ms. Coulter for a speech and learn from an American blonde who's willing to share her limited knowledge of international society with you in exchange for a bank account transfer. She'll tell you all you need to know about American immigrants in general, and Nigerians in particular, from her copy of *Heart of Darkness*.

Which reminds me: immigrants and foreign policies have long been a prime target for these "public interest" scam commentators and conservative con artists.

Wherever there's a government program in the US, there's a gigantic opportunity for self-aggrandisement by these fellows. A fair percentage of social commentators scamming the American public are only interested in the books they sell and the marketing buzz they generate—a much deeper concern for them than Medicaid or Medicare fraud.

Thus, Ann Coulter, in her own statements, has admitted that her views do not pretend to being balanced or fair—as long as she keeps getting the money she makes off the American public, she might have added. The lady is simply interested in making money off the American people—for contributing absolutely nothing to the public. Just take a look at the Ann Coulter website, and you have these gems:

> "*Never Trust A Liberal Over 3. Autographed First Edition*"; a book that is priced at US$28, coyly looking for buyers, in the finest tradition of writers everywhere.
> "*Booking an Appearance: Speeches and appearances can be booked through Premiere Speakers Bureau. College speeches can be booked through Clare Boothe Luce Policy Institute or Young America's Foundation.*" Just so you know that Ann Coulter comes highly priced, but she's also willing to give a discount when sales are down.
> "*She is a frequent guest on many TV shows, including Hannity, Piers Morgan, Red Eye, HBO's Real Time with Bill Maher, Fox & Friends, Dr. Drew,*

Entertainment Tonight, The Today Show, Good Morning America, The Early Show, The Tonight Show with Jay Leno, Hannity, The O'Reilly Factor, and has been profiled in numerous publications, including TV Guide, the Guardian (UK), the New York Observer, National Journal, Harper's Bazaar, The Washington Post, The New York Times and Elle magazine." And you can almost hear the webpage groaning at this elaborate name-dropping, job-seeking resume.

Those are statements from Ann Coulter's website. Autographs, speeches, interviews. Marketing for doing absolutely nothing. And she wonders who constitutes the liability to the American economy?

Do you notice anything that stands out about this marketing list? This is the kind of profile you will expect from a door-to-door hack salesman clobbering through the American southeast seeking an uneducated and ignorant clientele. She's quite the public scammer, this one. And even if she lays claim to being a native-born, it's quite certain that her ancestors were soot-faced labourers exiled from a European farm, probably for stealing farm implements.

Benjamin Franklin may not have recognised African names— he wasn't that gifted—but, at least, he must have known what a "coulter" was: a common farm implement.

Ann Coulter is certainly farming for publicity. Enormous, unwieldy, corrupt American government programs run by arrogant bureaucrats are bad enough for the Americans, but Ann Coulter and her ilk, milking American credulity, are even worse. But after decades of Americans paying for the upkeep of Ann Coulter and these other "public speakers", one can't help noticing that Medicare and Medicaid are beckoning Disneylands for these native-born social parasites.

But the problem isn't their social commentary; it's their ignorance and indolence. In Nigeria, we think only intelligent and reputable people get to lead public opinion. That's not true in America!

America, for example, leads the world in "public speakers," a job description just about as close to "unemployed" as one can get. Every level of American society is run amok with these creatures, with the smart ones getting money from international audiences, the mid-range ones getting national attention on Tea Party platforms, and the stupid ones spouting hate messages on the internet. At American universities, you can graduate with a degree and still be as oblivious as Ms. Coulter. The University of Lagos would have done the lady much more good.

Now, let's talk about Nigerians, the latest target of these conservative public speakers. It is irrelevant when any ethnicity—apart from the natives—started to settle in America. After all, there were only a few Caucasians in the Americas until the late 1600s. However, if there are nearly 250,000 Nigerians in the US today, then the US has benefited more from that relationship than has Nigeria. From the 1970s when the US was eager to lap up Nigeria's economic oil boom till today: these Nigerians—as well as other Africans— have distinguished themselves in sports, science, business and the arts. They contributed positively to the American economy until a conservative white president grounded the economy and a black president had to take over!

Of course, Obamacare never would have passed without the massive economic degradation of the Bush administration. But instead of opening their minds about their own problems, these conservative "public speakers" are seeking to blame American problems on Nigerians—a tactic that they have consistently used in the past. Nigerians are not concerned about Obamacare; its failure or success is, to put it mildly, irrelevant to Nigeria. But conservatives don't change their minds—they only change their scapegoats. In order to bash Obamacare, Ann Coulter and her friends had to bring in the Third World to shoulder the blame, displaying their crass ignorance of foreign relations and exposing the American public to international ridicule.

The downside is that America is now chock-full of people who, instead of looking inwards and understanding what America stands for—a cultural melting pot—prefer to cast away all national responsibility and blame others for their affairs. If the thought patterns of Ann Coulter and her ilk are anything to rely on, Americans are like a whining child, ready to blame everyone else for their problems.

Only a good knock on the head can reform such a mentality.

Gosh, I sure hope these parasitic American "public speakers" have Nigerian-style entrepreneurship, and are very keen on getting off their podiums and attempting an honest day's job for once!

Nigerians are now aware that a certain Ann Coulter is the Paris Hilton of American politics; we're just astonished that such a job description exists in the first place.

Random Flashes:
ON INFERIORITY

There seems to be this perception that you can determine a person's level of sophistication by their ability to correctly name car hire services in London and restaurants in Dubai. Especially with a—usually insipid—accent picked from these travels and which has somehow, suddenly dislodged the local one that has been in place for over twenty years.

This fraudulent social psychology is a fallout from the days when the most knowledgeable person in the colonial African community was the one who had shipped out of Africa—for education or otherwise—and had come back with marvellous stories of life beyond the black continent. Naturally, these "been-tos" attained oracular status, and thus began the craziness of modern Africans mistaking overseas travel for metaphysical knowledge or the possession of another country's visa as a statement of intelligence.

15

WITH MALICE TOWARDS TRIAL LAWYERS

Note: *Lawyers are, probably, an overpriced social commodity in Africa—and trial lawyers are, well, even worse. I grew up believing in the social value of trial lawyers until I actually became one and realised that the justice system had more to do with procedure than with substance. The first time I appeared in court before a judge, I was all a-sweat. I knew almost nothing about court appearances and not even my fine qualifications from both the university and the law school could reassure my nerves. Yet, by the end of the day, I was able to handle my appearance easily and smoothly—and I even had the opportunity to coach another lawyer on some finer aspects of procedure. How did I go from being a novice to being such a great trial lawyer in one day? And how can you become one with little or no formal training? All you need is the recipe that makes a person a trial lawyer, the stuff that separates these gods from laymen, and like the best things in life—these are surprisingly simple. If you can* *imbibe these few tips you are about to read, you might just be on your way to being the next Senior Advocate of Nigeria.*

IT HAS NOTHING TO DO WITH SCHOOL: The first big point is the fact that nothing taught at school is necessary to be a trial lawyer. Well, for the sake of legality, you can go through the 5 years + *x* (*x*, of course, being the number of years wasted by university strikes you have to factor into your plans) in the university, endure the rigours of the law school, the expenses of the call to the bar, and the miserable experience of having an unremarkable youth. But if you want to fast track your legal career (and, maybe, risk a jail term), or at least make a living as a lecturer to Nollywood courtroom scene writers, you need not go to study law. Just start with the next point.

IT'S ALL IN THE UNIFORM: You need a wig and a gown. These are basic. You cannot be a trial lawyer without a wig and gown. This is simply impossible. The Nigerian legal system has not evolved sufficiently to accommodate plain dressing. In fact, if you go to court without one, you become invisible. That's the truth. Ask any lawyer. You can jump up and down in front of the judge, dance the latest jig in town on the court seat, and scream for attention at the top of your voice. The judge can't see you, he can't hear you. You are absolutely invisible. But once you doff the good old wig, and the black flowing gown, well, you appear—yes that's the language—you appear before the judge. And if you need to disappear again, just take off the wig and gown.

Wigs—like the female species (apologies to the womenfolk)— manifest in diverse shapes, colours, and sizes, and you have to choose one with the same care with which you would take a spouse. You see, your wig is your legal partner; it is more important than the hair on your head, or your head itself. The judge is set up above so he can look down on the middle of your wig. He doesn't need your face. So you want to present a wig with a compelling character to the judge, a wig that makes the judge smile, one that makes the judge sympathetic. Your wig is your countenance. A great lawyer uses a great wig.

Of course, you've seen pictures of the tattered and battered wigs; don't be fooled, that's a sign of nobility. Those aged wigs are more expensive than you may think. They cost four times as much as a new wig and are only available in select stores. If you can lay your hands on one of these, you're a very lucky lawyer indeed and definitely on your way to greatness.

THE FORMULAS (WORDS AND PHRASES): You have to study, and memorise, the formulas that distinguish lawyers from the rest of the world. A layman, even in wig and gown, is soon spotted by a misuse of these phrases. Like an initiate into a coven, the skilled application of these magical phrase is what guarantees advancement. Let's examine some of the more important ones.

"Lords and Worship" It is a fatal mistake for you to address the judge incorrectly: men have been hanged for less. The judge is "Your Lordship" and he is "my Lord" and, whatever your religious beliefs may be, His Lordship doesn't give a care. My Lord has no gender, for the law is unmoved by feminist theories of language, and if you dare to 'my Lady" His, admittedly female, Lordship—well, don't.

"Worship" is used for the demigods, the magistrates; they are worshipped, like spirits, but not as fearfully as the Lords—who own you physically, emotionally, spiritually, and legally, once in their courtrooms.

You do not give pronouns when directly addressing these Worships and Lordships. Do not use "you", or "he", as this would be considered impertinent—bringing their worshipful and Lordships down to the level of men. Judges are beyond pronouns. These are not men (or women); they are super humans who hold the balance of life, death and your bank accounts. Consider this: even God reserves judgement for the end of the world, but human judges are less reserved, they deal judgement instantly.

"*May it please your Lordship . . .*" You use this phrase when you have to introduce yourself to the judge, especially when you have just 'appeared' before the court. Not "please, sir", or some other layman variation. *May it please . . .* you are begging (beg, dammit!); you do not want the judge to dismiss your appearance or ignore your wig. And if the Lordship refuses to be pleased, you are done for, your goose is cooked, and your case is struck out.

"*Serve*" has nothing to do with servitude. In the legal world, "serve" is a command. You serve people with documents, not with actions. If you want your neighbour in court to answer a case—you serve him with a writ of summons. *Serve your neighbour as yourself*; Jesus would have advised, if he was a lawyer. If you are served with a writ, then serve a statement of defence as well. Go ahead, also, and serve the witnesses, serve the experts, and serve everyone else involved in the matter (including wives, friends, children, pets, and the judge—if he gives a decision against you at the end). If you would be a leader among lawyers, you must first learn how to serve.

"*Respectfully*" and "*due respect*" Do not confuse these two. You use 'respectfully' when you know you really need the judge's favour and you want to show your humility as humbly as possible: "respectfully appearing", "respectfully move a motion", "respectfully about to go to exit to the toilets before I commit gross contempt in the face of the court!" On the other hand, "due respect" is a phrase reserved for those rare times when you are cocksure of your footing and you don't need anyone's blessing to proceed. This is when you are certain the other lawyer, or the judge, has goofed and you want to gleefully point this out, and in the most annoying manner possible: "with all due respect, my lord will recall that I told you the same thing last month", "with all due respect to my learned colleague, he seems not to have studied the facts of his own case", "with all due respect to the honourable Supreme Court, what the hell were they thinking?" Let's put it this way, there is no respect in a "due respect".

"*Move a motion*" Never forget: you have to move your motion. Never mind that it is called a "motion", in reality, it is always seated in one spot "before the court" like a stubborn ram refusing to participate in a fight. If the judge is to do anything with the inappropriately called "motion", you have to—move it. To move the motion, you have to "*rely*" on an affidavit (affidavits are the lawyer's best friend) and maybe a "*written address*" (Whether postal, web, email—so far as it is written). Your opponent will try to prevent you from moving the motion, and he will "serve" you with a counter affidavit, and other annoying things. Do not be dismayed, whatever you do—move it.

YOUR BIG BAG: You should get a big, heavy, briefcase. The kind of briefcase that creates the impression of strength when you hold it. Black is a good colour—it matches the robes. But the magnificent lawyer goes for oxblood—just because the colour doesn't match the robes. Imitation leather is fine; no real lawyer spends on genuine leather. In any case, get a big bag, for this is what tells the judge and other lawyers that you are around for serious business. You cannot make a BIG name for yourself without a BIG bag. Stuff as many books as possible into your bag. It doesn't matter whether the books are relevant or not. A text on applied chemistry popping from the bag will make you more distinguished. The form of the bag is what matters, not the meaning of it.

Don't forget, the practice of a trial lawyer is all about *appearance*.

PART THREE

CRITIQUE

Restating the Obvious

There's Always a Junction

There's always a junction
Where remnants of the night's sacrifice
Welcome fast the morning traffic

And there a voice calls from the road
The wail of a lunatic messenger
Crying out his morning dispatch:

"Cursed are your politics
Who stray from Obatala
Lord of mankind and all man's nature

"Cursed are your vehicles
You who forsook Ogun
Who breathed your machines

"Cursed are your cities
For Olokun is angry
And his aquatic army ranges

"Cursed are you by Sango
For his lightning is dire
And your houses in darkness

"Cursed is your counsel
Ifa withdraws his wisdom
And rots you in ignorance

"Cursed is your harmony
Shattered by Esu
Violent lord of mischief

"Curses on your days
Slaves of alien ways
Ensnared by deceit . . ."

And the voice fades away
As the traffic deepens
With sacrifices for the day

There's always a junction
Where lunatic words are shaped
And then flung north and south

16

EVERYTHING IN NIGERIA IS GOING TO KILL YOU

THERE ARE TWO THINGS YOU need to note: first, the title above is not panic propaganda. Of course, it sounds like one, talks like one and smells like one, yet it's no propaganda, it's a fact. But even if you disagree with this premise, then let's call it propaganda, but it is one that has become necessary and urgent at this point.

Second, I'm quite serious about the intent stated in the title: *Nigeria is out to kill you.* The country is going to hell in a hand basket. This is not a drill. And we have arrived at this point simply because you don't care. If you understand this statement, then you need not read any further.

Are you still wondering what this means, or how we got to this point? There are many articles with superb analyses of the current crisis. These have listed all the factors responsible: from an incompetent president to malevolent and influential sponsors of terrorist activities. But the singular—if remote—cause of Nigeria's current situation is this: we stopped caring about Nigeria. At a point, we gave up on our government and country and became irrationally selfish.

Look, the struggle for food is real. Surviving in Nigeria today has boiled down to the ability to fill your stomach—literally and metaphorically—and the stomachs of your family members, I get that. I'm a part of that struggle. I earn my living as a lawyer and I try every day to live comfortably on my livelihood. Nigeria has no plan to feed you and you have to sort yourself out. I have no arguments against that in principle. Except this: *you still have to care.*

And here's what happened to me last night: I had just read about the new bomb blast in Abuja—almost immediately after reading an email from a client in Asia. The client's email was important—and as a professional, my response should be immediate and devoid of emotion. After all, money must be made.

But yet, at that moment, I was possessed of a wild madness, for—within the larger scheme of things in Nigeria today—that email, the client and every other money-making channel is as self-sufficient as a bottle of water floating in a flood. I turned off my phone and went to bed, angry. Why? Because it doesn't matter how much I earn individually when my safety to earn the money is no longer guaranteed.

And that's the bad news: the Nigerian nightmare has changed. Nigeria has evolved from "*not taking care of you*" into "*actively trying to kill you*". Human-induced deaths are intensifying. And as far as a reasonable layman's analysis can be relied on, things are going to get worse. Much worse.

The Igbos had a taste of this concept during the Civil War. They understood the idea of a country being out to kill a portion of its citizens. Also, Nigerian society in general has also experienced this minutely, in the deaths caused by bad roads, fake drugs, faulty constructions, poor health service and other substandard government services. Experiences that propelled us to, individually, search for alternatives from private sources or migrate to the care of foreign governments.

But these deaths at the hand of poor services are insignificant compared to what is coming for us now. Corruption kills slowly, but bombs and guns don't waste time, viruses don't discriminate. Things have escalated now, and both the government and the opposition have nothing to say. Nigeria is going to kill us all—and this is not a metaphor.

Unless you start caring.

You have to understand that the Nigerian struggle is no longer about feeding your family. It is *now* about keeping your family from being killed. Write this on wall: the struggle has changed. Nigeria isn't just a corrupt country anymore; it is now a dangerous country. And if you don't change your thinking and actions along with this fact, you are going to die—or someone close to you will.

And no, prayer isn't the answer now—if it ever was. If prayer is your thing, by all means, pray. You're going to need that confidence builder. But don't mistake the tranquiliser for the cure. Just as you install a car alarm and fasten the locks on your gate, you will also have to take some physical or mental action before you get killed by Nigeria.

And there's more bad news: you can't secure yourself by isolation. You can scramble to the top of your career all by yourself, you can fill your bank accounts by your own game plan, in fact—you don't need any help to get up and about in life. *In life.* Everything you're doing right now only makes sense because you expect to be alive in the next few minutes. But your safety is no longer a valid proposition.

And this is unfortunate because you can't prevent yourself from being killed—all by yourself. This is why man invented society. Because isolation is dangerous. Countries exist, principally to guarantee safety.

But now, your country is out to kill you.

Unless you start thinking seriously, and start caring deeply, about Nigeria's fortunes now. Nigeria will kill you unless you start caring.

Look, you don't have to love Nigeria. You don't have to love this government or even love your fellow Nigerians. Love is a different issue entirely, and the gods know Nigeria—and probably your neighbour too—has done nothing to deserve your love. Love is a higher calling, it has to be earned. No, you need not love Nigeria. But you need to care about Nigeria. The same way you care about your education, the same way you care about your religion, the same way you care about your career, the way you care about your favourite sport or hobby. You have to reorient your priorities and place Nigeria at the top of your care list.

And if you still don't understand this, then you are the problem with Nigeria. And you deserve to die by its hands. You are too involved in your private battles that you are no longer in touch with the big picture. You can no longer see the wood for the trees. You're so caught up in your aspirations to become the main salary earner in your company that you forget there will be no company without a functional legal system. You bury your head in the sand of your goals and delight in your private accomplishments. Well, boardroom battles, market strategies, classroom troubles, bedroom issues—these will all vanish when the proverbial shit finally hits the proverbial fan. And the said shit has piled up.

You have to start caring now.

And no, caring isn't a tweet or two; caring isn't a Facebook like or simply sharing this article; caring isn't your anxious expression of concern while discussing at work; caring isn't just the 15-minute prayer topic in church.

Caring is your conscious and active engagement of the realities of your society and government through the exertion of your physical, mental and material resources.

See, society won't transform itself magically. There is no "society" out there, waiting to do as you say. Society is the collective identity of individuals. And if the individuals don't care, then society doesn't care. And that society will be destroyed. If you cannot stop what you're doing today—if you cannot stop it for a second and take some time to reflect on how your actions will restore some sanity to Nigeria—then you are the problem with Nigeria.

But you don't care. And so Nigeria is going to kill you.

And so, by all means continue to grow your cassava and your maize, pass your exams, do your job, earn your daily bread, pastor your churches, lead your prayers, teach your classes, fill out all those forms, strike that new deal, reply all your emails, and chase up those clients.

But unless you already have an exit plan for when things go to hell, then you might as well go to an undertaker and book your coffin today.

Because: everything in Nigeria is going to kill you.

Random Flashes:
ON BOKO HARAM

Now, of course, the Boko Haram menace is no longer "a pressing issue" in the country. It's now a fact of existence.

Seriously, every well-bred Nigerian knows that a situation stops being a "pressing issue" after three days of non-resolution by the government. And, after two weeks it stops being an issue altogether. And accordingly, the most successful public policy of Nigerian governments has been: "Hang on; let's just allow this one to blow off by itself."

Common sense says Boko Haram isn't going to blow off by itself, and an offering-load of prayers will not resurrect one dead victim. But this is Nigeria, and we love to screw around with vital situations. And that's why the government is committed to investing prayer into public issues. And as long as the Nigerian government continue to muddle personal spiritual issues with public policy issues they will continue to screw up the job they are given.

17

THE UNCRITICAL CITIZENS

INTRODUCTION

URING THE DARK AND HEADY days of Occupy Nigeria in January of 2012, a roadblock was mounted by some community citizen protesters at Pako, a minor junction that connected the traffic from the Yaba, Somolu and Bariga axis. As was my irregular practice in those days, I would first stop to provide some moral support to the barricaders at Pako, and join in stoking the angry bonfires at that junction before commencing the trek to the main protest grounds at Ojota.

On one of such days, I arrived at the junction to discover a dispute in progress. A local cabdriver, coming from Bariga, was attempting to cross the barricade into Akoka with his *kabukabu*. His intention was, however, thwarted by the irate protesters who insisted on his turning back towards his originating point. Their argument pivoted on the premise that the driver was knowledgeable about the general strike before he set out on the road. The driver, a man of good physique, verbally gave them as much as he got.

I watched the argument with mild amusement. The behaviour of the protesters was, however, not irrational. By some undefined criteria involving the use of common sense and their best judgment, the protesters allowed some vehicles with legitimate business to pass while they turned back others. The driver succeeded in arguing his case and he was allowed to pass. He then drove his car into the road where I stood, and from which I had been observing the proceedings.

Having safely gone through the barricade, the driver got out of the vehicle and walked back to meet the protesters, brimming with a fair amount of righteous indignation. In summary, his admonishment was that he had no problem with the Occupy Nigeria protest, but he had a problem with the road barricades. He started to berate the protesters for their physical activity and urged that they disbanded and left the streets. At this point, I walked up to him and challenged him. It was one thing to stand aside from protest, I said to him, after all every person had his own quota for tolerating nonsense; but it was another thing to start discouraging those who did speak out in protest. The man stared at my fragile frame from his great height for a few seconds, no doubt considering a finely angled slap. Then he turned aside, went to his car and drove off. An uncritical citizen.

That incident, as well as several interactions on and off social media, has made me consider the nature of those citizens who are neither interested in social reform nor care about its incidences. The non-critics. Who are these people? What disillusions them?

THE RESIGNED MAJORITY

In Nigeria, these are the people who have given up on their right to demand good governance and the expectation of social good. They believe they have seen protests come and go and that all politics is an unending cycle of evil through which the individual has to create a path within the social construct. Accordingly, they consider social crusades as pointless. Considerably comprised of the late '50s to early '70s generation, these Nigerians have lived most of their lives under the brutal administration of military regimes, the devastating effects of civil war and the horrors of a post-oil boom economy. To them, democracy is an end in itself. The disappearance of military rule is considered as relief enough. They expect nothing more from democracy than the fact of its existence.

Their position evokes some understanding: if you have lived in a world where an uneducated soldier could freely and publicly whip a professor, the fact that such a soldier is back in the barracks becomes a worthy achievement. With the death of Sani Abacha and the transition to civilian rule in the late '90s, these non-critics thanked heavens for a military-free Nigeria and left the civilian government to do as it pleased with the philosophy that a bad democracy was always better than a benevolent military.

If you were to call these category of non-critics out to protest or to advocate social reform, they will simply pity your ignorance. The problem, however, is that such people think only of themselves and their present comfort—not the future welfare of their children. These are the bulk of non-critics who epitomise the concept of the happy, suffering and smiling, cowardly Nigerian; people who would rather adjust the boundary of the wall than push back for what they rightly deserve.

THE LIVE-AND-LET-LIVE FOLKS

Closely aligned to the Resigned Majority are the "Live-and-Let-Live" folks whose stand on government policy is always tolerance. They have no age bracket and a number of Nigerian youths fall into this category. Their philosophy comes, not from any experience with government brutality, but from an innate belief that government service is a job that can never really be done right—and that "trying" is good enough. Some of these people are of the opinion that excellence can never really be achieved by human endeavour, and only some form of divine intervention can really make things right. It is a fair bet that you will find a good number of religious leaders within this group.

Accordingly, these Nigerians believe that public officers should be treated like the bright but wayward child of an indulgent parent—hand him some sweets when he does well, and reprimand him good-naturedly when he misbehaves, and nothing else. These non-critics believe that, occupying the same shoes, they would probably have acted the same way as the public officer in question. Naturally, they are prone to disagreeing with people who preach that reformation is possible. Human nature is necessarily fallible, they will counter, and since government is comprised of humans, one should not expect too much from government—either functionally or morally.

But this is where they miss the point: in the process of time, the indulged child will realise that the reprimand "lacks teeth" and that he can get away with as much misbehaviour as he fancies. Once the opportunity for discipline is lost, the child grows impossible to control. Fortunately for parents, with a child, this analogy is flawed, as circumstances can be remedial—the forces of life can impress discipline into the child without much ado. With a government, however, the situation can only worsen—no government voluntarily does the right thing—until an unappeasable force finally controls the excesses of government.

THE COMPARISON BRIGADE

What I call the Comparison Brigade refers to the apologists of incumbent government who, ordinarily critical on social issues, become defensive of an incumbent government and then gauge any criticism of a current government by the failures of previous governments. Usual with these "incumbent" non-critics are phrases like: "What did Obasanjo achieve in 8 years?" "Did Yar'Adua provide 4,400 megawatts?" and so on. They tend generally to look backward and consider criticism of government as an indictment either on the ethnicity of the public officer or on his capacity to achieve what other governments did not achieve. While their facts, of which they have many, are valid, they are generally fallacious to the arguments involved—as they do not help in reaching valid conclusions.

Most of these people are party members, and they are as defensive of their public officers as those Christians who confuse their pastor with Jesus. But a political party should encompass common ideology; not generate a personality cult. Loyalty to the party isn't the same as defending a misbehaving party leader. The non-critics of this category prevent social progress on the belief that a call for reform is an automatic degradation of the incumbent public officer.

THE SYCOPHANTS

Their name speaks for them. They are indifferent to manifesto or philosophy, belief or ideology. They are only interested in self-sustenance *via* their ranking within the corridors of power. These non-critics are out to fill their pockets from the coffers of "any government in power". Accordingly, they will praise, idolise and genuflect before any public officer who is in a position to satiate their lust for money.

Their loyalty is, however, fleeting. If perchance, they criticise a previous government in their support of the current one, then their criticism is suspect; they would eagerly cut the throat of the public officers they worshipped yesterday if it would somehow benefit them today. These people are despicable, and generally, nothing can change their nature.

CONCLUSION

One of the poignant lessons I've learnt as a social crusader is that not everyone sees social issues from the same point of view, which is fair. For every person who supports a view you hold, there is always another person who opposes it. However, some social issues are as evident as a fact proven in court, and it is only people in the categories above who do not see it as worth pursuing. It is more disheartening that there are Nigerians who, not being critical, would further malign the social reformer who has taken time off his schedule to analyse the way forward without prospect of personal gain.

Of course, a number of supposed social critics are merely interested in advancing themselves to positions of power, which, when obtained, they turn 180 degree, and show their backs to the very philosophies they previously advanced—these are not the persons whose support I advocate. I refer instead to the work of those disinterested persons who set out as watchdogs for their societies and expect nothing in return.

Nigerians ought to learn how to criticise the misdeeds of their governments, and support those who see it as their duty to do so. It is not until this sense of responsibility has been awakened that the much touted phrase: *the voice of the people is the voice of God* will start to make some practical sense.

Random Flashes:
ON FAITH

The ability to define one's self accurately is the starting point to achieving one's goals. You should know the difference between one thing and another for, as the philosophers put it: A = A and nothing else. A society in which perception and reality are confused with each other is going to be a damned inefficient one.

Today's society, stimulated with the Pentecostal idea that faith is a key to achieving anything, has gone gaga on this principle, way beyond the intentions of the original teaching. And so, for faith, we substitute a confused misrepresentation of reality, and define our circumstances through our perceptions while shutting out the facts.

But in the smart words of Jesus, "Suppose one of you wants to build a tower, won't you first sit down and estimate the cost to see if you have enough money to complete it?" Now, that's a thought on being realistic.

18

#Bornomassacre
A 22-Point Outcry

Note: In February 2014, even more unnecessary violence was unleashed in Borno in the unending terror that has traumatised the North-East of Nigeria. I wrote out a few points in reaction.

1. A time comes in the evolution of any country when it becomes necessary for its citizens to take stock of the national affairs and frankly assess the suitability of the men and women who have been empowered as the proprietors of the nation's undertakings.

2. This examination is necessary. Continued disinterest will, eventually, culminate in the unavoidable destruction of the socio-political system; the inherent weaknesses of the social construct will become uncontrollable and the entire edifice will give way, resulting in what is conventionally called, a failed state.

3. Nigeria has come to that point where an examination of the government is urgent.

4. It is, probably, unfortunate for Goodluck Jonathan that he is the current president of Nigeria at this period. In fact, he is not personally responsible for the distant causes that have created the current state of events. Nevertheless, he is, as sworn and willing president, obliged to shoulder the responsibility of the immediate causes. Goodluck Jonathan may be a well-intentioned person, but the road to hell—as is commonly stated—is paved with good intentions.

5. The road to hell has been set out before Nigeria today. The consequences of Nigeria's historical and current socio-political choices are observed in the following statements: (i) **Politics**: the country is gradually dividing along predominantly ethnic lines, with the minority ethnicity in favour of the incumbent and a majority in opposition, both of whose political representatives are equally determined to hold power in the next elections; (ii) **Corruption**: is on a rise, several allegations of public corruption and reckless financial decisions have trailed the current administration, even more importantly these allegations have been made in varying degrees by a former president of the country, the speaker of the House of Representatives and the governor of the country's central bank; and (iii) **Security**: the North-East of the country is gradually disintegrating into a lawless territory, one practically controlled by the *Boko Haram* outlaws and where children can be easily kidnapped or killed under the full glare of a supposed military occupation.

6. These facts are disturbing, and none can be dismissed without repercussions. The year 2015 is bound to be an interesting year—if not a terrifying one—for Nigeria's politics. The political situation alone, is a topic worthy of several outcries—but the most important, and the most urgent, assessment, *right now*, centres around the violent occupation of the North-East by *Boko Haram* and the continued helplessness of the Nigerian government in the presence of this crisis.

7. Nigerians need to decide *now*: do we prefer to kick aside a failed government or do we want to risk a failed state? This is no rhetoric: the Nigerian government has lost control of the security of the North-East, and possibly more. And the consequence is clear: a government that cannot safeguard the lives of its people is no government—but a useless sham, and it ought to be jettisoned as promptly as possible. Economic and political misdemeanours can be forgiven, but a security lapse is non-negotiable. The guarantee of the right to life is the barest minimum service a government can provide its citizens. Political and economic participation may be limited, social amenities and welfare may be non-existent, but the right to life cannot be joked with by *any* government.

8. It is clear that every Nigerian has a right to life, and that it is the duty of the Nigerian government to ensure the protection of this right—at all costs, and by all means. This duty by the government—this duty to ensure every individual's right to life—is weightier than budgetary allocations, it is more important than the financial systems, more urgent than election calendars, more

serious than cabinet meetings and definitely more necessary than any commissioned project.

9. However, the Nigerian government has no sense of duty. Instead, the Nigerian government mistakes its duty for the singular acts it does dispassionately from time to time. This is quite wrong.

10. The government's duty to ensure the right to life of every Nigerian does not mean a mere *condemnation* of an attack on Nigerians.

11. The government's duty to ensure the right to life of every Nigerian is not simply about securing a *location*.

12. The government's duty to ensure the right to life of every Nigerian does not simply mean deploying soldiers and policemen to a location.

13. The government's duty to ensure the right to life of every Nigerian does not simply mean imposing a curfew on the citizens.

14. The government's duty to ensure the right to life of every Nigerian does not stop at the declaration of a state of emergency.

15. The government's duty to ensure the right to life of every Nigerian does not include organising or requesting religious prayers.

16. Instead, the government's duty to ensure the right to life of every Nigerian is a philosophy; a functioning, breathing aspect of every government policy. It is a duty that addresses every *individual* Nigerian—not just locations in Nigeria. The government's duty requires the government to be—and be seen to be—unambiguously in pursuit of an all-inclusive security policy. It requires that every domestic action of the government, every foreign and diplomatic relationship, every budgetary spending is underlined by this security philosophy. This duty requires the *physical* and *personal* presence of the government in an affected area—with the affected *people*. It requires the suspension of every non-essential governmental activity until a violent situation against Nigerians is resolved. It involves the prioritisation of government spending on the relocation and rehabilitation of affected citizens. It involves an unequivocal stance, constantly repeated and steadily acted upon, that the life of the Nigerian citizen is non-negotiable, non-*amnestiable*.

17. This requires a government that works.

18. This requires a government that does not blame domestic violence on international events; a government that does not substitute spiritual philosophies for security policies; a government that understands that there is no government without a people.

19. Is the current administration such a government? I don't believe so. The Nigerian legislature is, of course, as bad as the federal executive, but one arm must be used to discipline the other—and then be chastised by it in turn.

20. The current Nigerian government has to be jettisoned. This government has to go, lest your children become the next victims of its inefficiencies.

21. And we—you—cannot afford to wait till election time to do this while the North-East—and all of Nigeria—burns.

22. You know what to do.

---·❖·---

19

WHY ARE WE PROTESTING, SEF?

An Occupy Nigeria Justification

SOMETIMES, IT REALLY GETS CONFUSING

EVERYBODY IS TALKING.

Some people are shouting. Others are carrying placards and others are burning tyres. Some are writing articles. Others are analysing figures on TV. At least, one person is dead. Why is there so much noise?

The President says we are hoodlums. We, the protesters say we are educated folk. Frankly, you probably don't care either way. There are more important things you have to worry about. You have a stomach-ache. Your lousy boss has been testy all week. Your final exams are just around the corner. Your wife is nagging you more than ever. Your child is sick. Your husband is cheating on you. I understand. These are serious issues. Everything else is just noise. If the President wants to increase the price of fuel, it's his business. After all, this will not be the first time pump prices have been increased.

But this is not just about the fuel price hike. Forget what the newspapers say: most of them are manned by people just as confused as you are. This is about life. Life in Nigeria. You see, all of your issues, one way or the other, are connected to this country. They will get better or worse depending on how this country fares. And if there is a war, you will forget about your problems instantly. We do not want a war to happen. We simply want to protest.

I have walked in protest and carried my placards. It was not fun and the threat of violence from the police was in the air. But I did it, anyway, and I will do it again. Now let me try and explain to you why I had to do it.

REASON 1. POLITICAL: WHEN WE SAY NO, THE PRESIDENT MUST LISTEN

The President is not the political boss. We are. He has four years to spend after which we will kick him out or allow him a second tenure. The people are the bosses of the President and he has to listen to us. If we say: *Mr Jonathan, you must not do this.* Then he must not do it. We don't care about the economics of the issue. Our No is No. He should listen to us first before listening to his advisers. We voted for him. Not because he is the smartest, but really, because we liked his name and his history. If he feels differently about it, he should try to convince us—not force it on us. If we keep quiet about the matter, it is one thing. But if we kick against it, it is a different thing. If he decides not to listen to us, we can tell him to shape up or ship out. Don't forget: we, that is, you and I, are the President's bosses.

REASON 2. ECONOMICAL: THE MATH DOES NOT ADD UP

Let's forget that we're the bosses, let's be considerate and look at the economic issue. The problem is that the economic issue is very complicated. It is advanced economics. So, let's simplify it with a story.

There was once a family of one father and several children. The father had inherited land from the grandfather and held it in trust for the children. The land had tenants on it and brought in money. As there was a continuous flow of cash into the house, the father resigned from work and let his businesses die. Unfortunately, he was also a careless spender, a drunkard and a glutton who lived luxuriously while his children suffered. His only effort towards taking care of the children was to allow them take some of the crops which grew on the land, so that they could eat twice a day. He ignored their schooling; they wore shoddy clothes and had no playthings. But the children ate what they could from the land and learnt to fend for themselves.

In the course of time, the father got into debt and realised that the income from the land was not enough to accommodate his expensive lifestyle. He thought hard on how to keep up his lifestyle and maybe start a few new projects. Then it hit him! A lot of money could be saved from the crops the children have been taking from the land for food! So instead of cutting down his expenses or getting a job, the father decides that the children's food is the problem. The children eat too much from the land. In fact, they should start paying for what they take from the land.

And that is what removing the fuel subsidy is. It is a story of selfishness and greed.

The government—our hypothetical father—has tried, and will keep trying to "educate" us on how the money saved from what they plan to take away from us would help in developing the country. *But we don't care about the economics, the math still doesn't add up.* We are not scared to say that out loud.

REASON 3. PHILOSOPHICAL: NO MORAL RIGHT TO DO WHAT'S RIGHT FOR US

It's true, sometimes the people are wrong and the leader is right. In such a case, the leader has a moral right to do what is best for the people despite their wishes. But moral rights are not automatic, they have to be earned. Even parents have to earn the moral right to dictate to their children. A vagabond parent cannot suddenly sermonise to his children. Our leaders have not earned that moral right. He who preaches equity must come with clean hands, the lawyers say. Our leaders do not have clean hands; they have fat pockets and grabbing hands. Until the individuals in government are stripped of their wealth, they have no moral authority to ask the people to donate to the common cause.

REASON 4. PHYSICAL: "WE" OUTNUMBERS "THEM"

We are more than the government. The government has decided to introduce its policy by force and we will also resist it with force. In fact, we do not want the government to rescind the policy willingly— we want to *force* it to rescind the policy. We want the government to realise that power belongs to the people.

We do not fear the bullets and the tear gas. The police and soldiers are humans too. They will either join us or they will get mowed down. We will resist the fuel subsidy removal policy and when we succeed in that, we will demand for more. Yes, we will.

This protest is not about the fuel price hike, it is about us, the people, shaking off the government, like flies from our back and rising up until we drive them back to their garbage dumps. If all of this sounds forceful to you—it is because we have been pushed too far.

FINALLY

Don't be afraid to come out and protest. You are doing it for you and for your future. Otherwise, fellow Nigerian, why not just take the next flight and migrate to the UK? They will welcome you as a second-class citizen.

So You're Too Smart to Protest? I Agree!

A Social Plea

The President is Not Better than You Are, or Maybe Not

I HAVE A FEW WORDS FOR you.

After spending about seven hours walking in protest on the long, hot highway from Yaba to Ojota, I went back home cramped and tired. I got to my little kitchen and discovered insufficient cooking gas. There was nothing else available to eat. I grabbed a can of beer and crashed on the sofa, hungrily wondering what the hell possessed me to go out protesting the fuel subsidy removal in the first place.

In fact, I could accommodate the financial effects of the subsidy removal. It would cost me some more thousands of naira in my monthly budget. I would have to reduce my savings. My dependents would be forced to accept less than usual from me. But I have a fairly comfortable job, and like the President sermonised, in the long run, I would adjust my lifestyle to the new way of life.

But why should I adjust my lifestyle to the new way of life? Why not the President himself?

Come on, you say, the president is *The President*.

Oh, I see! But I have a few questions too.

The President has a more generous kitchen budget, but does his family have better and more expensive taste buds than mine? I don't own a car, and he has several—does his body have to be carried around in separate pieces? When I fly, I go by Dana, Aero and Arik; he flies in several luxurious "presidential" bomb-proof aircraft—is his life more precious than mine? If he wants to enjoy all of these, then let him do as I do! Let him work his ass off 8am to 6pm daily in a private sector job! Then he will be entitled to the fruits of his sweat and not that of the Petroleum Profits Tax.

But if you think the President is clearly God and I am a mere mortal, then, fine. You are right. I should not protest against God—I will adapt my own economics to the new reality.

But how about those who have *only* enough to eat, how do they adjust to the new reality? Why not let us just save ourselves the trouble of killing them in the long run and just do it now and fast? Let's just round up every family that lives on less than N300,000 in a month and every individual that lives on less than N100,000. We will put them in concentration camps and have them shot in batches. It will be quicker and less expensive. Think of the benefits! We can clear the commercial buses off the road and have them plied by private cars alone. No more stinking markets, just shopping malls. No more street beggars, no more hungry relatives. It will be just like the paradise promised by religious teachers! Indeed, the President is God!

Economists are not Hungry People—Except Your High School Teacher

Wait a bit, you say. This is about advanced economics.

Of course, it is about advanced economics. There are few things that confuse an average human being more than advanced economics. Even economists are stumped by advanced economics. Now, throw in African, plus Nigerian, add illiterate and a dash of religious—and you get the perfect combination of naïve and ignorant. With a citizenry where that combination is in the majority, you can get away with anything in the name of advanced economics. So the President gambled on this factor and he's planning to get away with his retarded economic policy.

Luckily, simple economics on the other hand is what it is—simple. *Question 1: You have N1000. You know if you spend above that you're broke. If you spend below that, you can save something.* You decide whether you want to be broke or not—either way, you know what's cooking. It's so simple primary school students can solve it using basic arithmetic. We may be confused by advanced economics but we are experts at simple economics. Simple economics tells us that the subsidy removal will leave us broke. As a test, let's give the Minister of Finance N50,000 and have her manage it as a livelihood for a month without going broke, then maybe she'll understand the true meaning of simple economics. My mother does it every month without running into debt. And if my mother says she can't do this with the subsidy removal, then that does it for me.

I am tired of getting smoke-screened by the so-called economic benefits of subsidy removal. I agree there is a benefit somewhere for someone (and maybe even for me if I know where to look), but I do not want to suffer to get *it*—especially when *it* is an undefined and non-specific theory. At least the Israelites knew they were getting "milk and honey" not just "benefits". So to hell with these economic benefits. The only person who can convince me otherwise is my high school economics teacher on minimum wage.

Anyone not on a budget of less than N80,000 *per* month should shut up about the benefits of fuel subsidy removal. Anyone in a tailored suit who doesn't shut up about the benefits of fuel subsidy removal should be stuffed in a drum of petrol and sent down the River Niger.

You May Be Too Smart To See the Obvious

Just in case the economic benefits theory convinced you and you're feeling smarter than us ignorant folk who can't do calculus to save our limbs from being torn to pieces, hang on a bit.

See, I agree with you. The subsidy removal is economically correct and IMF-sanctioned. Maybe my mother and a few other financially unfit persons would be killed off. So what? Charles Darwin had already written that this was inevitable in life; we're only adding a new twist to it. *The Survival of the Financially Fittest.*

Now how about you? Would you trust a swindler because he makes sense? The longer you look at a 419 scam the more sensible it becomes. Always trust your first instinct and walk away. The first instinct of the public is that this policy smells, and it smells bad. To you, this may look like the best idea since Lugard invented Nigeria in 1914, but government ideas always look that way on paper. Every time. 1960 to date has not been bereft of ideas. But sometimes, ideas can be a distraction from the obvious.

What's the obvious, you ask? One, the fuel subsidy removal could be a graduated process—you start with 5% and work it over to 100% over 5 years. For every percentage removed, equal social development is set in place. Two, if we need to encourage hasty foreign investment, all we need to do is remove the legal and tax bottlenecks imposed on doing business: we reduce fees for governor's consent, reduce stamping fees, reduce capital gains tax, reduce NAFDAC and other agency fees, reduce customs duties, reduce a hundred other fees! Three, if we need to conserve money, then we should split the budget of the legislature into half and then subtract another N100 million from it!

Obvious things!

Too obvious!

But I bet if they did all that, you and your family will stop benefiting from this oil money too. Right? So my family and I suffer instead? Not likely.

Try and Be an Average Nigerian, Just For Today

But let's forget all of the above. Let me just plead with you.

You're smart and rich, or maybe daddy pays the bills so you don't give a damn about the protest. Maybe you're like me—not wealthy by any standard, but economically comfortable. But, think of this: how many people like yourself do you *know*? They can't be many or they won't call your social circles "exclusive". Then think, how many like yourself do you *see* around every day? Fewer. For every two people in a car, there are thirteen more people in a bus—and that's just an arbitrarily generated fact. Even if you live in the fortresses of Maitama or Ikoyi, you are surrounded by gardeners, househelps, drivers, salesgirls, and others who don't have your physical comforts.

Forget the big business owners you rub shoulders with, it is their employees and the small business owners that matter in this protest. No one has asked you to donate your money to other people or increase staff salaries. No, you have a right to your money. This is not socialism or communism. This is about public funds and government spending. It is about popular demand. It is about democracy. It will not hurt you to lend a voice and more.

But it will hurt all of us very much, if you do not.

Random Flashes:
ON COWARDICE

As nice and commercially inclined as pre-colonial Africans were, they were also fierce warriors and soldiers, defending their wives and property with the fury of a castrated Don Juan. They honoured and even encouraged death on the battlefield, and a woman who had lost sons or a husband to war was a proud one. Cowards were ostracised and anyone who was not prepared to die for his land was considered a bastard.

But, despite their solid patriotism, these Africans lost the wars for their land principally because of lesser firepower and the mischief of the cowards and scoundrels among them. In obedience to the laws of natural selection, the brave and stubborn ones died off with their brave and stubborn genes, while those who accepted European authority went on to become the educated Christians or tolerated Muslims. And because, whether cowardly or brave, people will always reproduce their genes, today the descendants of the survivors are spread across the continent. Essentially, almost every post-colonial African today is a progeny of one of those cowards or scoundrels that gave up their land—rather than die.

We are the sons and daughters of cowards and scoundrels.

ENOUGH OF YOUR SIRENS, ALREADY. MY EARS HURT

To: The Military Officer
Who on the Third Mainland Bridge
Blew Past Me with a Blaring Siren

Dear Sir:

Re: Enough of Your Sirens, Already. My Ears Hurt

I refer to the incident on the Third Mainland Bridge this morning, a very common incident, too common, in fact, but still very annoying despite its commonness. I refer, sir, to the effrontery with which your convoy bullied me, and several other drivers, out of the road. I refer to the manner in which, Moses-like, you parted the thick traffic of the Bridge at the command of your sirens.

Of course, I understand your haste, traffic should not be a hindrance to the military man on his way to wage war at Ikoyi—I've been told that the gunfire and artillery shots in the officers' mess can be heard for miles around. I quiver to think of the men at the Obalende frontlines, the men who would perish if you arrived too late to sign some cheques. I hear the battle is raging fiercely in Victoria Island as men wait for you to come in and sign all those documents. Ah, the travails of defending the country! Ah, the toils of saving our lives from the menace of expensive prostitutes and the rising cost of beer! I understand your gambrinous hurry; after all, you could be facing a firing squad if you got to work late while I would only face a sack letter.

As you can see, I have gone out of my way to introduce myself as an understanding fellow. It's only fair that you should try to see my point of view as well. This letter intends to explain that perspective. In summary: *please turn off the siren and join the queue.* Yes, I understand that you are in a rush, but so am I—and a hundred thousand other people. You have important work to do, but so do I—and a hundred thousand other people. If I could, I'll take flight above the insanity of the road, but since nature has not deemed us fit to have wings, I'm willing to take my turn. It would be a mad, weird world if I were to fix a siren on my Honda and chase everyone out of my way.

Of course, you are a military man, with a big gun and several men around you—and I suppose you think this qualifies you to a right of way? Maybe in 1996, it would have, but not in 2012. That's why you ultimately take your instructions, not from the man with the biggest gun in Abuja, but from a man I'm capable of sacking every four years. But a military needs discipline—and the "take it or leave it" attitude you display is highly improper. It makes it difficult to support you. So, listen, if your boss is my boy, I don't think you should be strutting around. You're important, but not that important: you are the guy we pay to guard the gate. Security guards, sir, should not blow sirens in the living room—except in a period of emergency.

Well, I suppose we both have different ideas of what constitutes an emergency, but let me give you a quick guide: an emergency involves life or death—strictly so. No metaphors. If nobody is dying around you, and there's no likelihood of people dying anytime immediately, kindly depress the mute button, wait your turn in traffic and don't kill people with heart attacks.

Because, that's what you do! You increase environmental and biological tension, induce high blood pressure, stimulate hormonal imbalance, prompt cardiac arrest, and even cause accidents! Come on, officer! You're supposed to be defending me, not killing me! I hear your siren and my heart races to 440! It's a dog's life already— jumping out of bed at 5 a.m., bleary-eyed and with aching joints; having to start up the generator or stumble around in the dark, eventually wearing two colours of socks, joining the morning traffic—without you adding hypertension to the parade.

Maybe you just love the noise—like boys with firecrackers, maybe you are tickled by the sight of cars hurrying out of your way, maybe you don't even give a damn, whatever your reasons—it's fine. However, we can't always have what we want. Now, here's a warning: guns or not, whips or not, juvenile, trigger-ready men around you or not, I won't get out of your way again. You, sir, are a man like me, same flesh—same blood, same response to virus and bacteria, and same biological reaction to being beaten to a pulp by an angry mob. Please, do not let's get to that stage: you may have the guns, and whips and boys—but I have the people, the harassed and angry people you dismiss out of your way like so much chaff before the wind.

Meanwhile, keep being cheerful. A happy solider is a good soldier. Don't worry, nobody will attempt to assassinate you, it's not like you hold nuclear launch codes or something. Next time we meet on the road, I expect you to join the line and queue behind me. Enjoy the view same as I do, it reduces anxiety. I won't move out of your route and I would encourage other drivers not to move out either. Let's not smash each other's faces over this small issue, ok?

Regards,
Ayo Sogunro

2 2

ENOUGH OF THE
MILITARY ALREADY!
A Call To Action

THE CURRENT CRISIS

IN THE LATEST INSTALMENT OF the initiation of violence by a government against its own citizens, a mob of military men were deployed to forcefully dispel a protest for basic amenities by the students of Nasarawa State University. The use of the military in the circumstances was reprehensible in itself, and should, ordinarily, have given rise to a general hue and cry, but unfortunately, and much more gravely, four students were reportedly murdered by some of the soldiers when shots were fired by the military men at the protesting students. This is not just news, this is a crisis.

In a more civilised country, this wanton killing of unarmed students in such a fashion would be termed as the actions of terrorists, or of persons of unsound mind. In Nigeria, we call these instigators of violent murder "soldiers"—and by extension, "military men".

The Democratic Experiment

A Nigerian child born in the year 1999, when Nigeria commenced its current democratic dispensation, would be fourteen years of age this year—a teenager, fully conscious of the responsibilities and characteristics of a democratic government. Our theoretical child would be able to identify the concept of the executive, the legislature and the judiciary as distinct arms of government. The child would understand the electoral process and maybe even the concept of a republican representative government.

It would, however, be difficult for such a child to understand certain aspects of the Nigerian society as it fits into the democratic structure into which he was birthed and within which he has grown. These unclear aspects of society would include, amongst other things, the relevance of a soldier in a civilian setting—not just because this idea has not been explained to him, but also because the military machinery and its attendant imagery will not exist harmoniously with the rudimentary democratic concept the child has already formed.

An adult may try to explain to the child that the military presence is necessary for security purposes, but the inquisitive child will ask: what then is the function of the police? The adult may explain that the police are not well equipped enough, but the child will ask the logical question: why not equip the police instead?

However, the innocent logic of the child is lost on an adult Nigerian population that has lived, consciously, under the excessive force of military rule. To such an adult, the military was, is, and will always be a fundamental part of the governing machinery—either as a direct governor, or as an enforcement tool of the pseudo-democratic ruler.

The Psychological Damage

The interaction of the average adult Nigerian with the military has been one of oppression; rarely of security or protection. From the 1966 coup to the dictatorship of Sani Abacha *via* the Nigerian Civil War, the military has had a forceful presence on the streets of Nigeria. But unlike the policeman, who is bound (even if more in breach than in observance) by a criminal code and its procedures of arrest and trial, a military man has no rules of interacting with the civilian in a combat—principally because the military man is trained to regard any person he engages as an enemy and to use deadly force against the enemy.

A military man has no rules of civil procedure. He is trained to shoot, and to shoot to kill. Accordingly when the average Nigerian soldier goes on the streets, he sees the average civilian as a potential enemy—irrespective of citizenry or other factors. Unfortunately, the Nigerian military does not pay its soldiers with money or welfare, it pays them with power—the power to oppress Nigerian civilians.

Nigerians have learned this truth the hard way, and have managed to politely step out of the way of the military. The concept of "an officer and a gentleman" is reserved for the movies only. The best reality we have is the current democratic dispensation, one that involves an uneasy truce between the average civilian citizen and the military—and under which the civilian has the lesser bargaining power. For all is well with the civilian only as long as he keeps out of the way of the military man's sirens and convoys. But what happens to a student in the university? What happens when a Vice-Chancellor calls in the attack dogs and a collision becomes inevitable?

THE LEGAL SITUATION

Because the social psychology is biased in fear of the military's arms, the legal provisions are little enforced and largely ignored. Taking advantage of this psychological mindset, opportunistic democratic governments and their acolytes have continued to utilise the fear of the military to force the execution of policies that are not legally permissible.

The facts of what happened in Nasarawa are unclear at the moment, but in a country where it is possible to hire a soldier for the price of a bottle of beer, it doesn't take genius to figure out that someone with some form of civilian authority—whether the Vice-Chancellor, a local government chairman or even the state governor—called upon the nearest deployment of soldiers to contain the protesting students and consequently, had four students murdered in the process.

But is the current legal dispensation of Nigeria as fearful as the current psychological dispensation of Nigerians? Thankfully, the answer is "No". Our Constitution is very articulate in describing why we need an armed forces and what its components are. Section 217of the Constitution (a document still unfamiliar to most Nigerians) states that the armed forces would consist of an army, a navy, an Air Force as well as other branches the legislature may create.

The next paragraph of that section then describes the three functions of the armed forces: defending Nigeria from external aggression; maintaining Nigeria's territorial integrity/securing its borders from violation on land, sea, or air; and suppressing insurrection and acting in aid of civil authorities to restore order *"when called upon to do so by the President, but subject to such conditions as may be prescribed by an Act of the National Assembly."*

Unfortunately, as stated above, Nigerians have had more experience with the military in respect of this third function, than with any of the military's other responsibilities.

Even more unfortunately, the innocent dictates of the Constitution regarding the internal usage of the military are widely disregarded by both the government and private influential citizens. The Constitution is quite clear: before the military is deployed internally, there should be three situations in place: (i) it should be in aid, and not the supplanting, of the civil authorities; (ii) the military exercise should be by the direct order of the President; and (iii) the exercise must have legislative backing.

Any internal deployment by the military within Nigerian territory which does not fulfil these constitutional requirements is, from the logical interpretation of those provisions, an unconstitutional action, as well as an undemocratic one—the kind that merits the jurisdiction of a court martial and the imposition of severe sanctions.

THE FUTURE IS NOW TO BE DECIDED

Now, we have reached the lowest depths of the usage of the military within Nigerian territory. The Nigerian military has not just been incapable of protecting Nigerians; it has also continued to kill Nigerians. This is not just news, this is a crisis.

The tail continues to wag the dog.

The *Boko Haram* insurgence, the suppression of which should have secured the affections of the average military for the military, was widely unchecked until it became a full scale war. This failure, ordinarily, should shame any self-respecting military apparatus as they slink into the barracks. The Nigerian military has not improved the security situation of the average Nigerian—and has even shown itself incapable of guaranteeing its own security.

It has now become mandatory that all Nigerians begin to demand for a total return of all military men into their barracks. There should be no more military sirens on the streets, no more military men manning the premises of wealthy citizens, no more combat by the military against school students. It is time for the military to go for good!

In the present crisis, the President should immediately, and with good grace, issue an apology to the student body of the school and compensation to the families of the victims. Recently, the President's wife celebrated her "resurrection"—and the President should therefore understand the value of a single human life. The Vice Chancellor, or whoever invited the military, should be sanctioned. The officers who led the expedition should be court-martialled, and the soldiers who fired the killing shots should be convicted and executed—and yes, hanging is too good for them. But of course, none of these is going to happen, because the Nigerian government enjoys the death of its innocents.

But the fight against the military in Nigeria is not over. It is bad enough that our law enforcement continue to handle our laws as tools of civil intimidation, and not social regulation. Nigerians cannot afford to watch idly as soldiers murder students and an unruly military continues to invade civil liberties at different levels. Today, it may be some unknown victims in a relatively unremarkable school in Nasarawa, tomorrow it could come to your doorstep, with a friend or relative dying in your arms from a soldier's undisciplined bullet.

23

LEADING TOMMOROW
A Dissertation for University Students

WHY ARE YOU IN SCHOOL?

PERHAPS, YOU MUST HAVE ASKED yourself this question a number of times, "what the *hell* am I doing in school?" Don't be ashamed if you have no answer—getting an education in Nigeria is frustrating enough to create the type of scenario that seems aimless at the best of times and lethal at the worst. On the other hand, your life philosophies may be well-defined, and you may have an immediate answer to the question. Possibly, your answer may be the typical ones: you want to obtain a nice 2-1 academic class, graduate with a degree, and live happily ever after. Along the way and afterwards, you plan to pick up friends, connections, a spouse or spouses, a nice job, a lot of money, some religious credit, die peacefully and go to heaven.

If that's your ready answer, splendid! It's quite a nice picture, except—except that a lot of things could go wrong. Your lecturers may victimise you and prevent you from getting that degree, you might discover too late that your friends were available only for the fair weather, the job market may have undergone an economic depression, and your *connections* may, well, get disconnected. You might get desperate and frustrated; you may turn to the life of sin you didn't plan for, and die in disgrace or through a cruel death and, just possibly, miss out on the heavenly bliss you counted on as a last resort.

THIS IS NOT ABOUT YOU

I'm afraid I've painted a very gruesome picture in the preceding paragraph, but only the very unrealistic person will deny that these things do happen. The wretched rarely start out with the goal of living that way. Of course, you may be lucky—or divinely favoured, if you prefer—and have it smooth all the way, and then you may not. If you are not so lucky—it's largely not your fault, it's part of the social construct within which we live and operate.

I know a lot of lazy "ne'er-do-wells" mouth this same excuse of "it's the system" with bright justification, but such obvious interlopers aside, have you ever stopped to consider that there are quite a number of hardworking people who went to school just like you and who never "make it" in Nigeria?

More importantly, the economic philosophy of the governments we have had in Nigeria has made it quite difficult for the average citizen to achieve more than subsistence living: a day to day, hand to mouth, rumble and tumble sort of life. Therefore, you will have to find a good job or business by yourself but depend on friends and relatives before you get work, build your own house but live in rented accommodation, or with family and friends before that happens, and provide for yourself after retirement irrespective of whether you're capable of working or not.

Now, don't be mistaken: this is not a plea for socialism or communism; I believe in capitalism, as regulated by rational human interaction. And reason argues that no matter how free a market system is, where the basic elements of trade become so scarce, or resides in the hands of a few, the market is bound to become an oligarchy. Let us diverge a little here and venture into economics.

Assume, for example, that air has to be commercialised; it is apparent that, before long, in a free market, some people would accumulate a larger portion of air than others. You can't blame these wealthier ones: after all they used their productive efforts to obtain that volume of air. On the other hand, if some people, feeling a tad smarter, *stole* this air in order to resell it, or even some more others decided *not to sell* it freely at market prices, but to *hoard* it despite people dying, so they would sell it at the maximum price possible, then you can imagine further that, very soon the market would begin to die and, at the end of the day, other activities which required air for efficient operation will also fail and be destroyed.

Just like fuel.

You're a student, but you don't need to be a professor to relate my analogy to our social construct.

A STITCH IN TIME

You have witnessed this scenario at least once: the federal government increases the price of fuel, there is an initial commotion, but soon the citizenry accepts the new regime and things go on just as before. This reaction from the populace inspires the government to continue its performance. And the cycle never ends.

You may not be schooled in the intricacies of oil and finance, and you should not be concerned about attacking every unfavourable government action—sometimes there will be issues on which the government is right in its policy decisions even though negative in immediate effect. What you should be concerned with is the *reaction* of Nigerians in general and you, a student, in particular.

Nigerians are too accepting, too accommodating and too adaptive. But you have the power to change that. Even if you can't be revolutionary, you should not be a passive reactionary. In the ordinary course of a government–people relationship, some passive behaviour is necessary for the smooth running of society, but when a government has displayed a continuous system of taking the people's tolerance for granted, then the people are required to look out for themselves.

Now, section 14 of the Nigerian Constitution, which is still the supreme law of the country, regards the ultimate decision makers (sovereignty, is the word) as "the people", the citizens themselves. That's right. When it comes to final decision-making, the people as a whole have the last word. In Nigeria, as well as most countries, the people are generally: the elderly, the working class, the students, and the young.

WHO THEN HAS THE RESPONSIBILITY?

First, let us eliminate the elderly and the young from the categories of active people, leaving us with the working class and the students ("students" in this context refer to the students of tertiary institutions). These two remnant groups often overlap but are distinct.

Now, generally, once a person has joined the working class, the social construct forces he or she to be a pragmatist. Pragmatism, in the Nigerian setting, simply means, doing what you can to guarantee food on your table for as long as possible. The average working-class person is keen to find ways of buttering his or her bread—on all sides if possible, and except he or she is an idealist—generally considered a fool, all the slogans and cries that were chanted as a youth are forgotten, he or she joins the rat race and that's the end of the revolutionary story.

So, we can safely dismiss the working class from the group of people who will be responsible for changing society. We are left with the youths—particularly students who are at the stage where they can accommodate burning ideals without the worry of a family or the burdens of employment. You students, ultimately, bear the responsibility of directing the course of change in your country.

HISTORY'S LESSONS

Let's see what history has to say on this.

In May 4, 1919, about 3,000 students from universities in the Beijing area demonstrated in Tiananmen Square to protest against a certain treaty, the students marched on government offices and clashed with the police. In an age without Twitter or Facebook, the news of the student protests spread out and inspired boycotts by traders and workers' strikes. With the students and workers already in protest, the intellectuals were able to get into the action and proposed ways to stimulate Chinese nationalism, modernise Chinese culture, and strengthen the Chinese nation against Japanese and Western imperialism. This protest led to the new wave of Chinese nationalism that has affected its politics, women's rights, literature and economics—and led to the formation of the Chinese Communist party and has emerged in China's dominant role today.

In France, 1968, a lapse in the French educational system caused disquiet among students. Eventually, the Sociology students at Nanterre University near Paris occupied the campus, resulting in the closure of the university. With the closure of the university, the students' and teachers' unions called for a general strike and 9 million workers responded ultimately resulting in the government meeting the demands of the students.

Of course, you may have heard of the anti-war protests in the United States. In the 1970s student demonstrations against the involvement of US troops in the Vietnam War were common in the campuses of many American universities and colleges. At one of such protests, in Kent State University, the National Guardsmen fired into a crowd of students, killing four people and injuring nine. This incident triggered a nationwide student revolt. By 1971, there was widespread unrest in public schools across the country—the effects of these led to the end of the war and President Nixon's eventual resignation from office.

How About You?

A caution however: violence has rarely been a solution to any problem. It may sweep the problem under the carpet, but the problem is still there. Violence should never be initiated. In most cases, however, violence is initiated by the government—at that point, the citizens have a civic right to retaliate against their oppressors. A government that initiates violence against its citizens loses the monopoly of arms in the society; the people always have the right to take weapons and defend themselves.

From the examples I've given above, it is clear that at one time or the other, nations have found themselves facing an existential crisis, and it was the relentlessness of youths—students—that resolved the situation. I have shown you three examples: from Asia, Europe, and the Americas. You, a Nigerian, can set a trend for Africa.

It is possible you have protested against your vice-chancellor or rector on certain wrongs, but the vice-chancellor is not your problem, neither is the president of the country. Both the vice-chancellor and the president are as much victims of the social construct as the next person. The problem is the system and the problems it breeds, and it is this system that needs to be changed, the entire social structure, from the very roots. And this can be done legally too.

SHAKING THE LEGISLATORS

The senators and representatives *may* be hardworking, but we haven't tasked them enough. In fact they spend far too much time pushing themselves out of office—when we could do the job for them. You as a student have a better chance of monitoring the affairs of the legislature much more than the ordinary worker; you students can organise and execute the door-to-door collection of signatures required for the purpose of recalling an elected representative.

You complain that legislators rarely visit their constituencies, but they would respond fast to you when notice of such a move by the electorate gets to them. Now, if this exercise was co-ordinated by the student body and was happening all over Nigeria, in all senatorial districts and constituencies, don't you think any imaginable wish of the electorate will be met soon enough?

You may not be able to control the president directly, but when the seats of the legislators become too hot for them, they will control the executive on our behalf, as they are supposed to.

REQUIEM

There is more to say, but this is a time to act. Only you and your colleagues can prevent the present class of students from following the same pattern, graduating into the same working class and continuing the vicious system. When will you take action?

Random Flashes:
ON EDUCATION

It is true that, in a functional society, university education is not compulsory for everyone. But, in Nigeria, there are certain considerations to note. You see, Nigeria has integrated the possession of university education with the ability to attain a healthy middle class lifestyle. Consequently, higher education in Nigeria is, misguidedly, synonymous with having a productive future. Worse, this productivity complex is escalating into the requirement of a postgraduate degree and professional courses for career advancement. And in the absence of any social policies for those with minimum education, then tertiary education becomes a necessity for an average Nigerian.

Therefore, attempts by a government to increase school fees become, inadvertently or deliberately, an unjust marginalisation. Even worse, it is often unclear if such a government is keen on reforming the education sector or is simply trying to generate revenue. Assuming reformation is the intent, then there is a better way to do this. First, a hike in the fees should be gradual—not sudden, probably introduced to newly admitted students over a 4-5 year period. Second, a process for identifying gifted pupils should be established, so that these are not disenfranchised for lack of funds. Third, social and commercial policies should be implemented to reward technical and vocational achievements and not only academic qualifications.

Only after these are in place, can the non-academically inclined among us safely turn towards careers directly after completing secondary education and also approve an increase in university fees.

But as long as we keep handling the Polytechnic diploma as a lower grade of the University degree, instead of a distinct type of, and equal, qualification, we can't convince any student that university education is not compulsory for everyone to attain.

PART FOUR

CIVICS

Educating The Citizens

FLOWERING BUDS
Rotting chaffs
Of
Past harvests,
Stagnant farmlands and wilted gardens.
The darkness of a wasted age.

But dawn awakens
And
One stray glance reveals
Out of same wilderness:
Flowering buds
Here and there.

24

TO SADIQ ABACHA
On Behalf Of Wole Soyinka

Note: *Ordinarily, few Nigerians worry over the life and times of the scion of the deceased dictator, Sani Abacha. In a live-and-let-live economy, Abacha's children enjoy an enviable existence undisturbed by the average Nigerian. However, when one of them attacked Wole Soyinka for rejecting a national honour that had also been bestowed on their father, Nigerians were quick to dispense some advice to the children of the dead despot.*

Dear Sadiq Abacha,

I do not know you personally, but I admire your filial bravery—however misguided—in defending the honour of your father, the late General Sani Abacha. This in itself is not a problem; it is an obligation—in this cultural construct of ours—for children to rise to the defence of their parents, no matter what infamy or perfidy the said parent might have dabbled in.

The problem I have with your letter, however, arises from two issues: (i) your disparaging of Wole Soyinka, who—despite your referral to an anecdotal opinion that calls him as "a common writer"—is a great father figure, and a source of inspiration, to a fair number of us young Nigerians; and (ii) your attempt to revise Nigerian history and substitute our national experience with your personal opinions.

Therefore, it is necessary that we who are either Wole Soyinka's "socio-political" children, or ordinary Nigerians who experienced life under your father's reign speak out urgently against your amnesiac article, lest some future historian stumble across the misguided missive, and confuse the self-aggrandised opinions of your family for the perceptions of Nigerians in general.

Your letter started with logical principles, which is a splendid common ground for us. So let us go with the facts: General Sani Abacha was a dictator. He came into power and wielded it for 5 years in a manner hitherto unprecedented in Nigerian history. Facts that are uncomfortable for your family, but true all the same.

Now, for my personal interpretations: between 1993 and 1998 inclusive, when your dada was in power, I was a boy of 9 to 14 years and quite capable of making observations about my political and cultural environment. Those years have been the worst years of my material life as a Nigerian citizen. Here are a few recollections: I recollect waking up several mornings to scrape saw-dust from carpentry mills, lugging the bags a long distance home, just to fuel our "Abacha stoves" because kerosene was not affordable—under your father. I recollect cowering under the cover of darkness, with family and neighbours, listening to radio stations—banned by your father. I recollect my government teacher apologetically and fearfully explaining constitutional government to us—because free speech was a crime under your father's government. Most of all, I remember how the news of your father's death drove me—and my colleagues at school—to a wild excitement, and we burst into the street in delirious celebration. Nobody prompted us, but even as 13 and 14 year olds, we understood the link between the death of Abacha and the hope of freedom for the ordinary man.

These are all sorry tales, of course. Such interpretations would not have occurred to the wealthy and the privileged under your father's government, but they were a part of the everyday life of a common teenager under that government. The economics were bad, but the politics were worse. And I am not referring to Alfred Rewane, Kudirat Abiola and the scores killed by the order of your father. Political killings are almost a part of every political system, and most of those were just newspaper stories to us. In fact, I didn't get to read most of the atrocities until long after your father died. So, these stories did not inform the dread I personally felt under your father's regime. And this was true for my entire family and our neighbours.

Instead, the worry over our own existence was a more pressing issue. Your father, Sani Abacha was in Aso Rock, but his brutality was felt right in our sitting room. We were not into politics and we didn't vocally oppose Abacha, yet we just knew we were not safe from him. You see, unlike any dictatorship before or after it—your father's government *personally* and directly threatened the life and freedoms of the average Nigerian. Your father threatened *me*. And if your father had not died, I am confident that I would not be alive or free today. You see, over the ages, humans have consistently tried to shape the world to fit their beliefs—the successful ones are those who didn't need to kill for their intentions to be realised.

Think of that for a while.

Now, let's come to Wole Soyinka. **First**: you can never eradicate the infamy of your father's legacy by trying to point out the failings of another Nigerian. Remember what you said: A is A. Abacha is Abacha. And no length of finger pointing will wash away the odious feeling the name of Abacha strikes up in the mind of the average Nigerian. **Second**: Don't—as the musician sang—get it twisted: Wole Soyinka did not antagonise your father just because he was a military man—Wole Soyinka was against your father's inhumanity. Your father was intolerant of criticism beyond belief. Your father made military men look bad. Your father's behaviour was so bad it went back in time and soiled the reputation of every military man before him. Your father, finally, made Nigerians swear never—ever—to tolerate the military again. Soyinka may have worked with the military before—but your father ensured that he will never work with the military again. Do you see? **Three**: Evil comes in many forms: there is no qualification by degree. There is no "good" evil thing. Sani Abacha, Boko Haram, Hitler, slavery—they all fit into the same category of misfortunes. Soyinka is right: Abacha was just as bad as Boko Haram is—deal with it. **Four**: Soyinka has been kind enough to limit his criticism to the unenviable awards this inept government has given your father. But, you see, in a saner political system, we wouldn't just ignore your father, we would have gone one step further and expunged the Abacha name from all public records. Wiped without a trace. Abacha would forever be a cautionary tale against the excesses of political power. In a saner political system.

Abacha was brutal—and Soyinka was one of those individuals who gave us inspiration in those dark days. He was part of the team that founded the underground radio station to counter your father's activities. Let me rephrase in pop culture language: Wole Soyinka was the James Bond to your father's KGB. Most of the influential people either kept quiet or sang the praises of your father to stave his wrath. But a few like Soyinka spoke, wrote and even went militant against Abacha. But at the end, even Soyinka who never ran from a fight had to run from your father. That was how terrible things were. And now you want Soyinka to join the praise singers of your father? I'm not certain Soyinka has grown old enough to forget how he escaped your father, slipping across the border in disguise. You will have to wait awhile to get that praise from him.

Now, back to you. You have a deluded sense of your father's role in the progress of Nigeria's history. Nigeria has managed to be where it is today, not because of leaders like your father—but *in spite* of leaders like him. This is a testament to the Nigerian spirit of resilience, and our unwavering optimism in a better future. You owe every Nigerian an apology for daring to attribute this to the leadership of Abacha. Those "achievements" you believe were accomplished under your father were simply all the things he had to do to keep milking the economy, and thereby perpetuate himself in power—they benefited Nigeria only if, by Nigeria, you meant your family and your cronies.

Your tone is that of a white master who justifies his oppression because he clothed and fed his black slaves. That is what your father did. The fact that we choose not to regurgitate, and reflect on that socially traumatic period doesn't mean we accept it as your entitlement. We have not forgotten, and we will never forget. Sani Abacha raped Nigeria. *Your father raped us.* Your father raped us and then pressed some change into our hands. And he then tried to marry us forcefully, too. You may think all this is well and good—but then you've never been raped before.

But we now live under a democracy—the kind your father denied us—and so you are *free* to talk. And so you are free to insult the people who ensured that your father had sleepless nights. Had the revolution your father rightly deserved happened, you—and the rest of your family—would have been lined against a wall, before you could pen one article, and shot.

And we would probably have cheered.

But we live under a democracy now—a system of government where even the scions of former oppressors can talk, and write freely, about the benefits of dictatorship. That's a democracy. A concept your father wouldn't have understood.

Regards,
Ayo Sogunro

Random Flashes:
ON HEROES

There's a line of the Nigerian national anthem that's obviously there for the laughs. Actually, every line of the anthem seems to be for laughs, but this line is particularly extra comical: "The labours of our heroes past shall never be in vain."

The hilarity here is not that we have no heroes in the objective sense (we do, seriously) nor is it that we have consigned the labours of these heroes to the recycle bin (we have). The real joke is that our problem is much more serious: we have no idea what a hero is or who our heroes are. These days a number of odd figures show up on the hero radar, and so the word "hero" has lost all meaning and the criteria for selection have become quite jumbled.

The creepy value system most of us were bred with has blatantly encouraged us to regard getting millions of Naira in an effortless venture as a more worthwhile achievement than fighting social injustice without pay. That is why our leaders keep getting away with corruption. Because deep down, we value those who cram their mouths full much more than those who go hungry for us.

A people are defined by their heroes. Heroes are ordinary people who manage to do extraordinary things. Extraordinary things such as defending the weaker and battling the stronger. We used to have such heroes; some kickass awe-inspiring heroes who stood their grounds before teargas and gun bullets. We used to have men and women who stood and died for what was right. From the days of the Aba Women's Riot to the nights of Occupy Nigeria. We had voices that spoke without fear or guilt.

Yes, Superman and Batman used to live among us. But they are mostly gone now. What we have today are guys who win reality shows and rich women with oil blocs. These are our freaking heroes.

25

WHY YOU SHOULD BE WORRIED ABOUT NIGERIA'S ANTI-GAY LAW

BEFORE YOU PROCEED

TWO GUIDING PREMISES UNDERLIE THIS article. The first is this: this article does not support or reject homosexuality as a sexual orientation. The purpose of this article is not to plead the cause of homosexuality as a lifestyle—there are many who have done that, and this is no place to rehash the argument. This article instead recognises the existence of homosexuals as a distinct sub-culture—a minority, if you prefer—within a larger culture, and is concerned, instead, about a philosophy of hate and prejudice against this minority which is about to be set in motion in the guise of legislation.

The second premise is this: that you, the reader, are not entrenched in some belief system that supersedes any attempt at reason. And so, this article is not for those who rely on prejudice, and by "prejudice", I mean the bigots, the fanatics, the fundamentalists and all those who will support the stoning of a woman to death in the belief that she is a witch. It's a waste of time and ideas to attempt a rational discussion with a person whose fundamental philosophy precludes being reasonable. If you see yourself as one of these: Dear Sir or Madam, the following paragraphs are probably a waste of your time, and the insults you intend to hurl in the comments are assuredly a waste of your talents. You would derive more satisfaction by exiting this page now. The button is quite easy to locate.

However, on the assumption that you are the sort of person who resolves a dilemma through a sequence of rational principles; the sort of person who weighs consequences against actions, understanding the relationship of cause and effect, and has the ability to separate between similar but distinct ideas, then let us reason together on the superficial logic of targeting homosexuals in Nigeria through the following arguments.

THE LEGAL ARGUMENT

An average student of law will eagerly tell you that there is a clear difference between civil law and criminal law: he will explain to you that civil law "punishes" one person for his irresponsibility towards some other person while criminal law punishes the person for his irresponsibility to the state. If you have some time on your hands, a student of jurisprudence will inform you that there is a clear difference between law and morals, and while it is the role of the state to prescribe laws for the protection of the individuals and the state, it is the role of the society to prescribe morals for acceptance in that society. He could also tell you, if you care to listen, that there are situations where the goal of morals and law overlap in the same activity and that there are situations where the law says one thing and morals state another. If our imaginary student also has ample time, he could give you this example: if you are standing by a pool and you see a child drowning, you have no obligation to save the child, and you will not go to jail for murder—except of course, you pushed the child in. Society may call you a scumbag and you may forfeit your dinner invitations, but you are not a criminal as far as the law is concerned.

In case you are puzzled, the jurist will further tell you that basic role of law is—should be—the protection of the state and other individuals from the acts of other individuals or other states, and every other function of law derives from that basic premise. He will explain that as long as an individual has not threatened the welfare of other individuals, the law has no—should have no—problem with that individual. You see, jurists generally concede that the role of law (with the exception of canon or religious law as agreed to by the adherents of that religion) is not to dictate private action, but to ensure the safety of all persons and property under general parameters. Our jurist friend could give you another example: you can decide to jump off a mountain ledge in the name of sport— that is a private action. But when, in the name of sport, you push someone else off the ledge without his consent, it becomes a crime, punishable according to the gravity of the consequence of your push. Law, therefore, prevents harm to people who have not consented to an action, either directly or indirectly. Law does not—should not—decide on what your private action should be—that's for a Big Brother reality show. Public opinion should be left for the public, and a legal system should never, compulsorily, substitute a person's private opinion with that of the public.

But, celebrating a gay marriage is public, you may say. Let us not digress on the issue of whether a marriage celebration—gay or not—is necessarily public. In fact, let us assume that the marriage in question is celebrated just as loudly as church marriages are celebrated. But the law in Nigeria already takes care of that by declaring such a marriage invalid. If you are naturally antagonistic to homosexual marriages—if you think the troubles of a married life are the natural reserve of a heterosexual couple, then fine, the Nigerian law already invalidates homosexual marriage. But this issue is about *criminalising* what is already an invalidity. An invalid action is far different from a criminal action. Entering a wrong password to your account is an invalid action, hacking into another person's account is a criminal action. The gravity is determined by the damage it does to other people. A marriage conducted by a pastor in a Nollywood movie does not harm anybody, yet it is invalid— the law does not recognise it as a marriage, because it does not meet the legal requirements for a marriage. That's enough. Going further to imprison actors in a Nollywood marriage ceremony is just as petty as it is absurd. And this is exactly what the Nigerian legislators propose to do.

THE MORAL ARGUMENT

Maybe you are worried about your sexuality being doubted. If that is a worrisome issue for you, then let me reassure you: No, you do not need to be in support of, or approve homosexuality itself in order to disapprove of a law that sets out to make life difficult for homosexuals. Your heterosexuality is intact. You may relax.

This is a basic principle of conscience: just as you do not have to be black to fight slavery, or Jewish to be repulsed at Hitler's Nazi Germany. Justice defines circumstances—your stand against an injustice should be irrespective of the nature of the person against whom the injustice is committed. Opposing the Nigerian government on its prejudicial law does not automatically commit you to a life of homosexuality.

What you are opposing is simply the use of the law to target a group of people who pose no threat to the life or property of Nigerians. You may find a homosexual person intolerable, you may forget to invite them to your dinner parties and thanksgiving services. But when you target them for jail—or keep silent while this is being done—makes you no different from the Nazis of Germany and their hatred of Jews or the Apartheid whites of South Africa and their repulsion at blacks. You see, it's easier to sit down and criticise other bigots in history—but do nothing when faced with a similar situation.

But even worse is the criminalisation of associations that support or advocate gay rights. Any student of human rights will tell you that an attempt to ban people from discussing gay marriage or promoting it is just as bad as an attempt to lock up Arsenal Football Club fans. The Nigerian situation is not a joke, however, and I am confident that a court of law in no distant time will adjudge that aspect of the law as unconstitutional. It is bad enough to put homosexuals in jail—it is repugnant to natural justice to then try to muzzle any support for them. And your individual silence in the face of such an injustice is a tacit approval of its execution.

THE CULTURAL ARGUMENT

A common argument in support of the prejudicial legislation—and one infamously and misguidedly utilised by Mr. David Mark, the Senate President, stated that homosexuality is not part of our "culture". Let us ignore the obvious fact that Nigeria has over 250 ethnic groups with diversified cultures out of which at least one involves a woman "marrying" another woman, another involves a husband "gifting" his wife to a male guest, another approves raiding a neighbouring nomadic camp to kidnap a wife, and several involve a brother or son taking the surviving wives of a deceased as inheritance—let's ignore all of these disparate sexual and marital cultural phenomena and focus instead on the nature of culture. What we call "our culture" is not a set of fixed, written rules handed down by our forefathers in a leather-bound book. Instead, "our culture", like any other culture, is an interwoven set of constantly changing practices. Culture, a student of sociology will tell you, is constantly in a state of flux: it grows new ideas, it borrows from other cultures, it ceases some long-held beliefs, and it is forever changing. You see, the only permanent culture is a dead culture. Jackets and fast cars are not the African culture, but I am yet to see a black man going to jail for perfectly stringing a Windsor knot.

THE RELIGIOUS ARGUMENT

Arguably, the two major religions in Nigeria are against homosexuality—but what about those who are not adherents of the major religions? On the absurd assumption that every Nigerian is either a Muslim or a Christian, then why not let's adopt the full canon of the Old Testament and Sharia? You see, as an average bible student will tell you: every head will roll. From the Christians who enjoy pork and bush meat—despite the clear injunctions of Leviticus 11—to the Muslims who have a fondness for beer. The only people left alive will be the fundamentalists, and they will soon kill each other from sheer intolerance. We might as well speed up this process and hand over the reins of government to *Boko Haram*. After all, what these terrorists want is the criminalisation of sins and the banning of ideas from the "West". And if we now start deciding to criminalise our sins, then we are all convicts waiting to be sentenced. The words of Jesus are more logical: *he who has no sin, let him cast the first stone.*

THE POLITICAL ARGUMENT

The Nigerian democratic setup—in the words of Byron—is an aristocracy of blackguards. Like the Greek gift, the goal of the legislature is to secure the affections of the unthinking Nigerians through a diversionary illusion while plundering us through other orifices. Let us not be ashamed to call a farce a farce. The threat of *Boko Haram*—and now *Hezbollah*, the devaluation of the currency, the escalating corruption in the public service, the rising price of goods, the unavailability of electric power—and several more—are far more real and dangerous threats to the welfare of the average Nigerian than the marital issues of homosexuals.

Whatever your inclinations about homosexuality, your bank account has not diminished through the sexuality of a gay person— unless, of course, you set out to spend money on some deliverance mission, which then is your own fault, but let us not digress. The point can be shown to you by any keen student of political science: as a political goal, banning homosexual marriage is at the bottom of the list of resolutions for Nigeria's 2013. It takes a smug legislator, self-assured in the gullible nature of the average Nigerian, to hurriedly push through a law dealing with a non-issue to score cheap popularity while ignoring pressing matters.

IN CONCLUSION

And now, here's the worst part: if this law is allowed to sail through, it could be your affairs that will be considered criminal tomorrow. You use your left hand to write? Criminal. You squeeze your paste from the bottom of the tube? Criminal. You wear your wristwatch on the right hand. You criminal! The facts may be different, but the principle is the same. This law is a test by the legislature, a measurement of how much nonsense can be dumped on the public. Of course, it is general public opinion that there are a number of clowns seated in the legislature—those who attained their claim to law-making solely by affiliation with their political party and not through a personal resume—and there is a tendency to just ignore them. However, when clowns begin to create dangerous precedents, then it is time for the audience to get serious and put them in place.

Random Flashes:
ON DEMOCRACY

Democracy, in its capacity as a game of numbers, is good for making decisions about the allocation of communal goods and resources: these are, ultimately, "shallow issues"—in the words of Socrates. But when it comes to decisions affecting rights, justice, fairness and equity—aka "urgent human questions" in the words of Socrates—you just can't leave it to a game of numbers and the will of the people. Rights, however defined, transcend numbers. The question of what and how these rights are ascertained is a different question. But when some clever politician argues that the mere "will of the majority" in a democratic setting makes an action okay, then this fallacy is certain to get a fair number of people confused. But anyone who has ever seen a violent "majority" mob knows that the argument is absolute nonsense. A mob, whether legalised or not, doesn't care about "urgent human issues".

Democracy is not—and shouldn't be—a license for the majority to destroy the opinion of the minority. Or vice-versa. No matter how reprehensible the other side of the argument is to you. It's a simple idea, but most people fail to see it— because humans are essentially wired to be self-centred. And here's the moral: if the discussion is about roads, airports and election timetables, the "numbers democracy" works fine; but when the debate shifts to the repression of the minority, then the fact that the majority are in support still doesn't make it right.

2 6

WITH APOLOGIES TO MY GAY FRIENDS

An Epistle

Dear Gay Friend
So Recently Traumatised
By An Insensitive Law

OPENING LINES

PERMIT ME A COUPLE OF indulgences before I proceed. First, I use the term "gay" generically, mindful of the fact that this term is reserved specifically for that classifications of sexuality known as male homosexuality. However, throughout the course of this writing, allow me to use the word "gay" as a place-holder—for the avoidance of circumlocutory language—for that variety of individuals that includes lesbians, the bi-sexual, as well as transgendered persons—and who knows—asexual and such other category unfathomable by the primitive mind. Second, I have also used the word "friends" in the loosest connotation of that familiar word. Prior to this debacle of legislative authority, I have had very minimal contact with members of the gay community—such contact being almost always from afar, observatory and polite. I cannot claim to have experienced the social stigma you confront, or the psyche of being an external member of your own society. I can claim, however, an affinity in this respect: several times in my own life, I have faced the onslaught of majority decision-making, and stood my ground against the suppression of the minority. I therefore claim a kinship with your present plight. More fortunately, I have had cause, in the last few months to develop an informal acquaintance with Bisi Alimi, whom I respect for his moral courage in being able to speak out, virtually alone, in the face of social ostracism, and whose name will continue to crop up as long as this debate goes on in Nigeria. I have also been privileged, in the last few days, to interact directly with several members of the gay community as a direct consequence of my stance on the anti-gay legislation wantonly passed by Nigeria's legislature.

JUSTIFICATIONS

Having then spoken out on the subject once, and received corresponding accolades and censure, why do I now write this letter to you? Two reasons—one, because, there can't be too much discussion on the existence of an injustice, and two, because, I believe that someone, a Nigerian, has to offer apologies to you for the misguided reasoning of this generation. My first response on this issue was, I believe, a rational discussion aimed at the reasonable people in the Nigerian society. However, this issue is not an exercise in theory—it touches your lives, your real, flesh and blood, lives. I'm afraid our internet comments and barstool discussions rarely take cognisance of this fact—as we analyse the pros and cons of whether you deserve to go to jail or not as dispassionately as we examine a Central Bank monetary policy: *should Nigeria have a N5,000 note or not?* This writing is not a rational discussion seeking premises and building conclusions—I have done that already—this is an emotive response, acknowledging your anxiety and your uncertainty in the face of social persecution. This is a contrite testament. And now, I confess a selfish reason for writing: this letter is not as important to you as it is for me and my errant generation—a documented testament for latter generations, that in the face of communal disinterest, some of us were able to stand firm against this new face of fascism.

APOLOGIES: THE LEGISLATURE

The first beneficiary of this vicarious atonement is, of course, the self-glorifying legislature whose major goal in criminalising homosexual relationships is to deflect social attention away from their own ineptitude and focus it on your variance, your difference, instead. You have to understand the crassness of the legislature for you to accept my apology on their behalf. These are a group of people whose generic motto is "We first, the people later" and who consistently prove that their major interest is in the perpetuation of their own gratification and the repression of social progress. In a sane society, they will be driven out on the streets and flogged with whips, one after the other. But Nigeria is not a sane society. Even more, these politicians have not fed fat on the flesh of Nigerians by chance alone—they understand, calculatedly, the Nigerian psyche. The Nigerian psyche is easily distracted by inconsequential drama, instantly attracted to grand political gestures lacking in substance or principle. The politicians understand, and manipulate, the Nigerian psyche of forgetfulness—forgetfulness by Nigerians that this same legislature, suddenly inspired to reshape public morality, still consumes a substantial part of the national budget. They know that Nigerians, like the fabled entrapment of monkeys, will not let go of the handful of nuts they can grasp through the bottleneck, content to sit and wait for death, forfeiting freedom for a desperate taste of the murderous bait.

APOLOGIES: THE RELIGIOUS ONES

Next, let me apologise on behalf of the religious—both the bigots and the seemingly reasonable. The former simply wants your head on a platter and the latter wants to see you "converted"—by jail if necessary. Both of these, however, equally share the mantra that "homosexuality is a sin", one that must be wiped out, conveniently forgetting the fundamental right of man to sin. But if you must sin, they prefer that you fornicate, instead, like "normal" people on the hilarious theory that God can only comprehend consensual sex between an unmarried man and woman, but not consensual intercourse between members of the same sex. These morally upright Nigerians are, of course, the modern day adherents of those two imported religions that have laid claim to the African inheritance: Christianity and Islam.

Ironically, the fundamental theses of these religions—Salvation and Submission—are woefully misunderstood by these African adopters; these preachers lack true knowledge of the spiritual philosophies they supposedly imbibe. And thus, the Christians have substituted the doctrine of Salvation of the sinner for that of Persecution of the sinner, and the Muslims, forgetting their claim that Allah wills all, would not submit to the will of Allah regarding the existence of the minority, but would rather rework the will of Allah, fashioning it after the mortal interpretation of what this will is. *The death of my son is the will of Allah,* they say—but not so the sexual orientation of a fellow human being.

But beyond the spiritual ignorance of our scriptural jingoists, which is pitiful, is their historical forgetfulness, which is annoying. They have forgotten the facts of history: forgotten that their religions, now dominant, were once minorities, victims of persecution and oppression by the pagan majority of the societies they were birthed in. Common sense suggests that the person who has experienced a difficulty is more sympathetic to the travails of a new sufferer—but alas, our society turns common sense on its head and the former lecturer now oppresses ASUU, the former labour leader is now a dictator to labour unions, and the previously oppressed minority— now the majority—gladly suppresses other minorities, supposedly in the name of God. And there is more to be learnt from history: the growth of Christianity through supposed heresies: the papacy, divorce, female preachers, female dressing, abortion, tithing, definition of the Sabbath—an impressing list of issues that have made the church a haven for variant, even opposing, beliefs.

And this forgetfulness showcases the inherent hypocrisy of these sudden enforcers of God's will on earth—for they have found a new sin, one that, by default, they cannot be guilty of. *"Allah be praised, Halleluiah! I might be an adulterer and a cheat, but thank God, I'm not gay!"* Secure in their knowledge of immunity from this particular "sin", they proceed to make it a criminal offence, complete with jail terms and trials, misguidedly securing their admission to heaven by the persecution of a specific "sin" committed by a specific number of their fellow-men. They happily resurrect long-discarded passages of their scriptures and stamp it across their action as a validity of their holiness. Forget about Salvation and Submission, this is Hypocrisy and Persecution.

Apologies: The Activists

And now, let me apologise on behalf of the mute social reformers and activists—those vanguards of truth and justice who have suddenly found some other activity to occupy their attention in the face of the grossest miscarriage of justice since the annulment of the June 12 election in 1993. These activists, neither hampered by political selfishness nor religious fervour, unfortunately, have demonstrated an indifference to the ideals they grandstand—enjoying the present attention of the gallery, afraid to sacrifice their democratic popularity. *We are not gay*, they reason, *it is not our problem*, and hence they substitute circumstance for principle. They set aside the fact that the law is in the name of Nigerians, the legislature a seeming representation of Nigerians. They forget—or ignore—that the underlying principle breached by the action of the legislature is the same as that of Amaechi's stolen election at the governor's forum. Just as one does not have to be a supporter of the beleaguered governor to voice against the injustice perpetuated against him by the President's cronies, one does not have to be gay to fight against a social injustice perpetuated by the general public. These *activists* will watch an accused person burn to death in the market rather than rescue him from the mob. You see, it takes a strong person to fight against public opinion. Forgive them, for they simply don't have that strength.

The Social Ridicule

And here is the ridicule for the world to see: a society with a police force still struggling to combat dangerous crimes is willing and eager to add more burdens to the travails of the police. This society is now willing to have policemen spend hours and resources hunting down and arresting homosexuals, parade them through the court system, waste hours of judicial time, convicting and sentencing gay people, and then clog the prison system—not with hardened criminals, but with gay doctors, gay writers, gay musicians, gay activists. Nigeria, Gulag Archipelago of Homosexuals!

But what drives the social psyche on this issue? Some sort of international recognition at a dubious first? Nigeria, the "first" African country to treat the gay issue seriously? Fighting against an imaginary social menace, or responding locally to some international crisis? This is the work of a social psychologist and beyond my scope. However, this much is clear: this law offers only some temporary amusement for the country, and the usual pattern of forgetful existence will soon set in. Today's anti-gay hullabaloo will be forgotten in the daily struggle to place food on their tables.

YOUR STRUGGLE BEGINS

And this is where you should begin to gather your own strength and pursue the silver lining in this ridiculous situation. You have not asked for rights before, you have not begged to be adopted into mainstream society, you have always maintained your small but distinct corner. But now, society itself has precipitated a discussion on your rights. Now, we can sit down and sort what belongs to you and what doesn't. This law, as dismal as it makes your circumstances seem, is a blessing. It forces you to fight—and fight you must. And this is the hardest part of this epistle: this call to protest.

Study the proposed law and ignore its provisions, one after the other. Your right to civil disobedience in the face of persecution is intact. You must come out in the open and force the ostrich head of this society to look you in the face. This will be hard for you and definitely painful—but freedom is rarely handed on a dish. Go to jail, if you must—but never permit yourself to be grounded in your own land. Let those who advocate—in ignorant summation—that homosexuality is the western world's problem—simply because the homosexuals in the west have been more forthright about their existence—know that your silence is not to be confused with guilt, your invisibility not to be confused with non-existence. And so let them drive you into jail by the thousands, let them enjoy the spectacle of the arrest and trial of gays and their activists—let the Nigerian Gulag get populated, the same has happened in history: from Nero to Hitler.

Closing Lines

And that is what history teaches: even if you fail *now*. History has always proven that oppressors never last, and eventually, all oppressive policies *will fail*. Nature works towards freedom and equality, it is man that makes cages and wields power over others. You, my gay friend, go on and work on yourself—be as human as you can be, and keep aiming higher within and without this society. Borrow a lesson from the history of Christianity: all it took for that religion to transform from an oppressed and persecuted cult and become the international religion of the Roman Empire was the membership of the Emperor's mother. Someday, surely, Nigeria's blind majority would be faced with the inescapable conclusion that a number of the powerful members of their society, who dictate political and economic policy, are, in fact, gay. And therein lies your victory.

Random Flashes:
ON CONFLICT

Of course, you've read about the hilarious conflict between the neighbouring "kingdoms" of Lilliput and Blefuscu in Gulliver's Travels. *But it's easy to make light of the story when you are unable to apply it to current realities. There are lots of Big-End and Small-End issues that cause unnecessary friction in real, everyday life. Of course, it is proper to hold a belief and stick to it, but it is improper to force that belief on others. Even more improper: using violence or the threat of violence to force that belief on others. Only a club, tribe, cult and other exclusive society would require that everybody maintain similar beliefs. But in a complicated, admittedly messed-up world, such as we have today, belief systems have become way too dense and numerous for a summary conversion: and the best scenario is for everyone to share this limited space or blow up the world in the process of determining which belief should survive and which one must die.*

The world doesn't belong to anybody. You meet stuff here, you'll leave stuff here. And all the stuff you think you've built up forever can be blown off in the puff of a madman's nuclear bomb from a corner of the world you've never heard about. But as long as you've got to share this tiny portion of Space with other people, you have to be tolerant: history has proven that any attempt by a majority to dominate a minority for the purpose of forcing behaviour always results in disastrous consequences for everyone.

27

NOW THAT YOUR TEN YEAR OLD GIRL IS OF MARRIAGEABLE AGE

Note: In July 2013, the Nigerian Senate attempted to delete a provision in the Nigerian Constitution that defined "full age" to include a married woman below the age of 18 years. Senator Sani Ahmed Yerima, infamous for his child marriage, successfully opposed this attempt and the provision was retained. However, these actions did not go unnoticed and a storm, under the label "#ChildNotBride", gathered in the media and on the streets of Nigeria.

FIGHTING THE GOOD FIGHT

M ASS HYSTERIA IS A WONDERFUL thing to experience in a lifetime. That overwhelming sense of being a part of a larger emotion is one of the traits that particularise the human as a social animal. You will find it in prayer grounds, election rallies, football matches and popular protests. I have been a consistent partaker of that last category, considering myself a "barricade mounter" of sorts. However, sometimes, it is necessary to step back from the alluring hysteria and examine an issue with a dispassionately critical perspective, and maybe even—protest against the protests, not because the intentions are wrong, but because the direction is incorrect. The current problem and its attendant emotions is one of such incorrect directions.

THE HUE AND CRY

I have assumed that, at the time you are reading this, you are acquainted with the current social *palaver* manifesting in the form of a general outrage at the seemingly support of female child marriages by some not-quite-honourable members of the Nigerian Senate. At first blush, the very proposition of such an idea should propel you to exclaim in horror at the paedophilic tendencies of the average lawmaker. However, a proper understanding of the set of circumstances that led to—for want of a better word—this palaver, will show just how complicated the socio-legal circum-stances are. I will, however attempt to discuss the problem as briefly as possible.

THE NATURE OF THE PROBLEM

In addressing citizenship issues, under a generally unremarkable portion of the Constitution of the Federal Republic of Nigeria ("CFRN" for short), the law states that, should you be inclined towards that idea, you have to be of "full age" to be able to renounce your citizenship of Nigeria. "Full age", not being a phrase whose specification is universally agreed on, the CFRN in its wisdom set the bar at 18 years of age—with a condition: a married woman (whether or not she has attained said 18 years, the provision could have added) will be considered ("deemed" was the word used) to be of *full age*. This provision, along with the rest of the CFRN, was drafted and set into law in 1999—and life went on as usual.

THE ENTERTAINING PART

Life would have continued on its journey, but for an attempt by the Senate, for some undisclosed rationale, to remove this "married woman" addendum from the CFRN as part of the perennial and often ignored charade of constitutional amendment. At the first roll of the voting dice, the Senate obtained the two-thirds majority vote (compulsorily required for an addition to, or deletion from the CFRN); the addendum was deleted and the worthy members moved on to other unworthy matters. Again, life would have progressed uneventfully, but for the sudden light bulb that went off in Mr. Sani Yerima's head on the deletion of this "married woman" provision

YERIMA'S MEDDLESOME INTERLOPING

You may recall that our main antagonist, Yerima, had had the unprecedented effrontery to publicly showcase his alphamegamia; marrying a girl whose lifespan at that time was nearer to 10 years than 20. Somehow, Yerima made a tenuous connection between the "full age" addendum in the CFRN, Islamic matrimonial principles in general, and his own peculiar marital preferences in particular. Never too slow to exert his opinion over others, he forcefully required that, unconventionally, the Senate should take a vote again over this matter that had already been decided.

Somehow convinced by Yerima's dubious argument, the Senate President rolled the dice a second time, and even though the majority of the lawmakers voted again to delete the addendum, the required two-thirds magic was not performed—possibly because some Senators had, understandably, washed their hands off the proceedings in disgust at this waste of taxpayer time. How and why the voting pattern changed at this second round may remain a mystery, but the result was the continued retention of the "married woman" provision.

THE ALTERNATIVE SCENARIO

Now, by virtue of Yerima's agony over the proposed deletion, it is generally assumed that this provision was what gave him permission to indulge in his proclivity for juvenile brides. But, sentiments discarded, what is the importance of this provision in the first place? Let me explain through this roughly drawn up scenario. Take an Egyptian girl, fourteen years of age, forcefully handed over in marriage to an older man, let's say a Nigerian. Preferably, our Nigerian suitor is a former state governor with plenty of cash for the girl's parents and plenty of influence to silence critics. By general law, our Egyptian girl attains Nigerian citizenship as soon as she marries our man. However, she lives a life she hates, this barely mature girl, and every night she plots an escape from her horrible marriage.

Within a year, she manages to execute her plans, and she escapes to the United Kingdom, far from her husband's grubby fingers. But, fifteen years and alone in the UK is no joke, and the English authorities are not too kindly disposed to this funny state of affairs. The English want to send her back to Nigeria. She pleads with them that she's not a Nigerian. Well, your husband says you are, they reply her. Then she says, No! No! I renounce my Nigerian citizenship. Take me to Egypt, instead. She begs.

Now, the white folks are confused. So they call up their favourite Nigerian lawyer: You can only renounce citizenship if you're 18, the lawyer says clearly. Sorry, girl, they tell her. You can't renounce Nigeria, till you're of full age. Now, off you go.

And so they get ready to bundle her back to Nigerians, to the waiting whips of her grubby husband. Wait! Our Nigerian lawyer calls back on the phone. There's an addendum, he explains, as a married woman, she's deemed to be of full age and she's therefore free to renounce her citizenship. She doesn't have to go back to Nigeria, it's right there in the Constitution.

HERE'S THE SENSE IN THAT

What the law tries to do is simple: it tries to give a woman who finds herself in an early marriage the same rights and freedom as a person of "full age". This is possibly, so that she does not lose both ways—being married like an adult and yet being denied the freedom rights of an adult. This, you will agree is a noble intention. However, like all noble intentions, this one also paves the broad road to hell, and the law, inadvertently, gives the nod of legal recognition to child marriages. Maybe this was a deliberate ambiguity; it's impossible to say without exploring the mind of the drafters. However, at the very least, it is a case of terrible drafting.

One thing is clear, though, there is no purported Islamic, Christian or customary right to marry young girls being protected or granted through that provision. In fact, the girl in question does not have to be Muslim or belong to any custom to rely on its freedom. For Yerima to appropriate the addendum to the protection of the Islamic faith is therefore, gross ignorance at best, calculated misrepresentation at worst.

BAD COMPANY AND GOOD LAWS

But Yerima relied on it—and this has made all the difference. His reliance on, and the interpretation he decided to draw from the provision—that is, that the law allows him to marry young girls—is simply unfortunate. The Nigerian law protected no such rights, but it was too late. The sensational media picked the previously innocent provision, widened its loophole, attacked it as a tool of Yerima and forever ruined its reputation.

THE MORAL OF THE STORY

But what is the lesson in all these? This is the part that has mostly been overlooked by the outraged Nigerians: that we have a legislature that does not know its own laws. Let us count the mishaps of our fumbling lawmakers: First, a legal provision that ought to protect girls forced into early marriage was badly drafted to resemble an approval of early marriages; Second, ignorant of its purpose, the Senate tried to delete this legal provision, instead of refining it to be clearer in intent; Third, and worst, the Senate allowed a self-serving Yerima to hijack the law and declare it as a protection of paedophiliac intents, even allowing him to drag his religion into the fray, when he should have been quieted and educated.

IN CONCLUSION

We may call for the removal of the provision, ambiguity and all, but we would only succeed in throwing away the baby with the putrid water. Deleting the provision will not stop Yerima and his type—they will merely find some other excuse—in fact, a deletion will only deprive victims of child marriages from claiming certain rights. Public outrage should be geared, therefore, at refining the legal provision so that its true intent is clear, imposing stiff sanctions on people who commit paedophilia in the name of religion or custom, and setting a legal limit for the consensual consummation of any betrothal or marriage. Only then, would our current mass hysteria be properly channelled, and possibly effective.

Random Flashes:
ON RAPE

Most religious and social philosophies firmly place the blame for rape on the feminine portion of the human species— because, intelligence is neither spiritual nor cultural. But that mindset has found less ground today: women, having "wised-up" in this current civilisation, have, also, not been hesitant in throwing back the blame at the male of the species for being incontinent assholes. And so the blame game between male offenders and provocative females goes back and forth—because, intelligence is also neither masculine nor feminine.

But there's a third category of people who inspire the messed-up mentalities that justify initiating violence against women: women themselves. And by "women", we do not refer to the girl in a bikini; but to the general category of females who are the first to cast stones against their fellow women on issues of gender relations and violence against women. The women with the "serves you right" mentality. These are the women who promote laws that limit freedom of dressing and appearance, or promote ideas geared towards returning women to the Stone Age. But not all women are as straight-up treacherous as to sponsor a law against "indecent" dressing or promoting an association to suppress female progress. Most times, encouraging violence against women is effected in the most subtle of ways—through the wacky gender philosophies that women teach their children. Especially through the promotion of what Wikipedia calls, ideologies of male sexual entitlement. Children are born without any impressions of male and female norms; but society, through the parents, impresses them with relevant social discrimination.

This discrimination includes ethnic, national, race and gender types. And from a lay point of view, we can safely say that while fathers mostly indoctrinate the children in political discriminations, mothers are generally responsible for the ultimate mindset of the child in gender relations. Therefore, a male child who grows up with the impression that men are superior to women or that girls who dress expressively are sluts, available for his taking, will eventually mature into the kind of man who takes provocative dressing as an excuse to rape a woman—or even a young girl. And a girl who is taught by her mother that she will be raped if she dresses in a particular way will have no sympathy for women who get raped—or even accept the female role of subservience in rape situations. But no excuse can, or should be allowed to, justify rape. The mere existence of something does not make it available for the taking. But men in general and rapists in particular, may never understand the logic that a woman's body is her body and nobody else's, until all women begin to drum this fact into men.

A *woman's body is neither for her father nor for her broth-
ers, uncles, nephews, boyfriend, husband, society, or gods.
And the lesson is this: the more some women encourage the
idea that uncovered bodies are invitations to sexual abuse,
the more they give an excuse to rapists to commit atrocities.*

28

THE STRAIGHT NIGERIAN'S GUIDE TO THE NEW ANTI-GAY LAW

ONGRATULATIONS, STRAIGHT NIGERIAN, THIS ARTICLE is for your benefit. Now that the Same-Sex Marriage Act has been signed, you can breathe easy—or so you think. Well, not so fast—and the following paragraphs will explain why.

However, as is usual in my articles of this controversial nature, I will assume you are a reasonable Nigerian (maybe one who *hates* homosexuality a tad—or even a whole lot—that's fine) but not one who thinks stoning a homosexual person to death is some sort of divine injunction—or that armed robbers are preferable to lesbians. If you're the latter type of person, don't bother reading this article, there are more important things for you to do: like amending your new law to allow you to directly murder gays and rape lesbians and save costs on the whole jailing thing.

But for the rest of you, well-meaning, straight Nigerians, here are a few things that you should get—well, straight—about the new anti-gay law.

1. **THE LAW IS NOT ABOUT MARRIAGE:** Fine, the proper name of the law is titled "Same Sex Marriage Act" and the general rationale from the sponsors of the bill is something to the effect that "gay marriage" was a devaluation of African and religious *family* values and similar nice sounding ideas taken right out of the holy books: which ought to make divorce a crime too, though nobody seems to mind that. But don't be deceived by the PR, the anti-gay law is just that: an anti-gay law. As a matter of fact, homosexual marriage has always been invalid in Nigeria since British rule—this so-called innovation is simply about *punishing* homosexuality. Let's start with s.1(1) of the law: "*Marriage contract <u>or civil union</u> entered between persons of same gender is hereby prohibited in Nigeria*". Did you notice the "civil union" part? That means, even non-marital relationships are prohibited and criminalised. And just to drive the point home—in case you're still arguing from the "marriage" angle—the law goes on to describe "civil union" to include: "*independent relationships, caring partnership, civil solidarity pacts, domestic partnerships, reciprocal beneficiary relationships, significant relationships*", and a host of other non-existent types of relationships borne out of a level of paranoia that is matched only by the political system's level of corruption. In short, gay/lesbian relationships of any type are criminalised—whether marital or not. And this is why, before the President could even pocket his signing pen, Bauchi State had already arrested people under the fresh law. Did these people organise a marriage ceremony while the law was being signed? If

that is not proof that this has nothing to do with marriage, then you tell me what is proof.

And the next time some religious person argues for the law on the premise that marriage should be only between a man and a woman, ask the person: "Fine, but what about a reciprocal beneficial relationship?"

Whatever *the hell* that means.

2. THE LAW DOESN'T CARE ABOUT DETERRING HOMOSEXUALITY: See, ordinarily, an activity becomes worthy of criminal status when people keep reporting to the police that it has begun to affect them negatively. And so it becomes necessary to deter that rampant activity. Crimes don't come out of the blue—they are a result of problematic activity in a society. Well, this law is not *deterring* gay marriage because gay marriage isn't an activity in Nigeria. It's not even deterring gay relationships because gay relationships are virtually secret in Nigeria. Secret to the point of non-existent. Instead, it is a *witch-hunting* law—one that punishes people whose opinions differ, even if the said opinions are not causing any problems. The law is a solution to a non-existent problem. Take, for example, s.4(1): "*The registration of gay clubs, societies and organisations, their sustenance, processions and meetings are hereby prohibited.*" Meetings? Even armed robbers are not guilty of merely "meeting". A meeting—and nothing more—doesn't even hurt a fly. That's like jailing union leaders for meeting to discuss a strike—in a democracy. Come on, they were probably *meeting* to discuss how not to be gay in a homophobic country! The law isn't interested in the substance of the meeting; it is only interested in jailing the attendees.

And if anyone should be jailed for meetings that harm the country, it should be the Federal Executive Council!

3. The Law Punishes YOU, Even if You're Definitely Straight: Take s.5(3), which is probably the most unfair punishment ever given to anybody for just being nice to another person: *"Any persons or group of persons that witnesses, and aids the solemnisation of a same sex marriage contract <u>or civil union</u> or supports the registration of gay clubs, societies and organisations, processions or meetings in Nigeria commits an offence and liable on conviction to a term of 10 years imprisonment."* Here's the deal: You will go to jail for 10 years, because you were cool enough to look the other way when you saw women making out. Why? Because you supported a same-sex civil union. In short, you will get jailed for having an opinion differing from the government's opinion. You get jailed for being a reasonable straight person. Remember the "meetings" part? You will be sentenced to 10 years in jail for *supporting* a meeting. In other words: *report any gay/lesbian persons and activity or go to jail with them.* Don't forget, the law isn't limited to marriage—it affects other types of homosexual relationships.

Summary: This law also affects heterosexual relationships. Because God wants to see straight people sent to jail for refusing to be judgmental.

4. The Law Doesn't Safeguard You: Fine, so you're straight through and through. And fine, you have no problem about informing on gay people in your neighbourhood—in fact, you are positively excited about this particular civic duty. But what happens when YOU are accused by someone else? See, there are no standards of proof beyond being involved in a "civil union", a phrase whose definition means a whole lot of nonsense. Take s. 4(2): *"The public show of same sex amorous relationship directly or indirectly is hereby prohibited."* "Same sex amorous relationship". This means, kissing, hugging, hand-holding, or other forms of affectionate—amorous—contact between the same gender is now prohibited in Nigeria. If you think this is a safe risk, wait till you are arrested and then try to prove *otherwise.* Maybe, a judge may ultimately find you not guilty, but think of the Nigerian justice system, and you will shiver at what powers to investigate your sexual life has been handed over to the Nigerian police.

5. THE LAW IS SET UP TO VIOLATE PRIVACY: In case, you didn't know it, here's what s.37 of the Nigerian Constitution assures every Nigerian: *"The privacy of citizens . . . is hereby guaranteed and protected"* which is a principal reason policemen are not allowed to spy into your bedroom without a warrant. Now, instead, the anti-gay law states in s.5(2) that *"Any person who . . . directly or indirectly make a public show of same sex amorous relationship commits an offence and shall each be liable on conviction to a term of 10 years imprisonment."* Now, tie that law to the police powers of investigation and you will get the problem in at least 4 steps.

> Step 1: The law ordinarily permits the police to investigate and arrest a person *suspected* of committing an offence in Nigeria.

> Step 2: It is now an offence in Nigeria to *directly or indirectly* display same sex affection.

Step 3: The police (or someone else) is suspicious that you are committing this offence and the police wants to investigate your sexual life—to prove you're not gay.

Step 4: There goes your private life.

Now, repeat Steps 1 to 4. This time between a male police officer and a female suspect.

6. THE LAW IS PLAIN WEIRD, EVEN BY NIGERIAN STANDARDS: Just take the basics, simple definitions: the definition of *"civil union"* isn't closed, and can legitimately mean two girls sharing an apartment; *"amorous relationship"* is not defined and so even heterosexual greetings can be maliciously interpreted as the expression of a homosexual relationship; words like *"support"*, *"meetings"* are used carelessly without defined categories and exceptions; the burden of proof is not stated; the law does not provide for categories of unintentional or "inadvertent" offenders; and worse—it is a retrospective, and even retroactive, law—a type of law strongly disapproved of by our constitution. In summary, it's a very lazy law—the kind a mob will hurriedly put together just to legalise their murderous instincts. But, you see, you can't amend such a law to take care of these issues—because they deal with private matters that are difficult to enforce by the public without sacrificing people in the process.

And that is why every sensible legal system understands that what goes on in a person's underwear is not the business of the law—to the extent that the person hasn't dragged in an unwilling third party.

But Nigeria has never been noted for being sensible.

29

THIS RECEDING
SENSE OF SHAME

ONE OF THE MORE SIGNIFICANT political events in Nigeria's democratic evolution—and one which seems to have escaped general commentary—was the news from the Akwa Ibom House of Assembly: a news item which would have been amusing if it wasn't equally alarming.

Essentially, that state's legislature—in full mental capacity, one assumes—okayed a law which, amongst other things, provides a life salary to ex-governors and their deputies; allocates funds of up to N90m annually for the domestic upkeep of each past regime; allocates up to N150m annually for medical services to guarantee their continued physical ability to enjoy the benefits, provides for a "five-bedroom maisonette" to be built for these worthies (in Abuja or Akwa Ibom—because choice is important); and dashes out such other mind boggling emoluments that would make an average Nigerian conclude that the news story was a prank report—somehow overlooked by an overworked and underpaid editor.

This is not the first law of its kind in Nigeria—both Lagos State and Rivers State have crafted similar legislation—but this, by Nigerian standards, takes the prize for its outlandish provisions and brazen legislative emergence.

But, in the absence of any contradictory statement from the Akwa Ibom State House of Assembly, we have to assume the story is true. In that case, this is a worrisome situation. Not because a governor who has served effectively doesn't deserve his reward, but because this law violently contradicts the ideals of accountability—and ultimately bastardises the concept of democracy.

You see, democratic process suggests that the promotion of public welfare should be the first consideration in the allocation of public funds. Public money should be spent on the greatest public need. This is a very straightforward idea and requires little argument. However, in some exceptional circumstances, public resources may be allocated to private persons as a symbol of solidarity: for example, handsomely rewarding the bravest soldier at the war front, or giving an annuity to the composer of the national anthem. But these are exceptional cases—such private persons must have done something outstanding to deserve the people's money.

More importantly, even in these exceptional situations, the reward is given to the private individual by *the public* itself—conveyed, often, through public opinion on the subject. Any resulting law on the issue is, more often than not, a legislative expression of public feeling in the first place. This is how things should be.

And this idea of measuring public good against public expense is consistent with democratic ideas: public money should not be dashed out randomly, and definitely not just as the person in charge pleases. Nobody is expected to be paid just for showing up. Yet, this exactly is what has happened in Akwa Ibom: governors and their deputies will be paid just for showing up.

There is no underlying concept of rewarding good deeds in the Akwa Ibom law. The individuals who will take benefits under the law may have obtained power through a corrupt process. They may have done nothing significant or developmental for the state. They may have looted and despoiled the state. They may even have been downright malevolent. It doesn't matter under the law. If they served as governors or deputies, then they get paid. They get paid simply because they held an elected position—in a country where winning an election is already its own reward.

This, alone, makes the legislation wrong.

But, there is a more alarming aspect to the issue than its lack of an underlying entrepreneurial principle: if the newspaper accounts are correct, this law originated as a bill from the sitting governor's office. This is a critical aspect. The law did not originate from the people of Akwa Ibom either directly, through public opinion, or indirectly through their legislature. Nobody went on the streets of Uyo asking that ex-governors and their deputies ought to be taken care of. Nobody marched in Ikot Ekpene or Ikot Abasi to get this done.

Instead, as far as anyone can see, the governor thought up the idea and sent the bill to the House to stamp it with the toga of legality. And, as the infamous meme certifies drily, *"Darzall"*.

Therefore, one has to wonder if the governor of Akwa Ibom and his counterparts in other states have not finally discovered the loophole in the countless campaigns against corruption: *why should you go through the trouble of stealing public funds when you can simply enact a law to give you the money freely, directly and without account?* This flaw in the fight against corruption seems to have eluded a number of governments so far, but now Akwa Ibom has opened the door.

A sitting governor has essentially allocated public funds to himself and his club members openly and without blushing. It is bad enough when sitting governors name streets and buildings after themselves in unabashed self-aggrandisement, but this has taken the accountability game to a brand new level. This is legitimate corruption—or stealing, if you prefer.

You see, the fight against corruption, so far, has focused on sanctioning public officials for flouting the existing laws. And that is why people walk free when you cannot prove they broke the law. But what happens when these public officials decide to save themselves the trouble of trials, by simply changing the law—or at least, directing it to favour them? After all, if a law allows it, then it is not illegal—and ultimately, it is not corruption. This is the fundamental question: who controls the lawmakers? What prevents other governors or the president from pushing similar laws across? What stops them from making it legal for all government officials to take 10% off every government contract they authorise? What stops a governor from passing a law giving his children—or any other person he desires—a salary for life?

The only clear answer, in Nigeria today, is this: because they still have a sense of shame.

But Akwa Ibom is proof that our reliance on this sense of shame may no longer be enough. And that is why this news story is significant to our developing democracy: the existence of the Akwa Ibom law is evidence that Nigerians are yet to have any actual control over the legislature and, by extension, the executive.

Of course, we have the judiciary. It is possible that some indignant lawyer may challenge the law in a courtroom—and it is possible that, by some stroke of luck, he may win. But the judges are meant to interpret laws not make them. And what's to stop the lawmakers from directly weakening the judiciary—by law?

Laws should serve as an impartial balance between human activity, and not as partisan tools to be wielded by some against others. But, quite frankly: what's now to prevent our laws from being used as the tools of oppression?

A sense of shame. Maybe. A receding sense of shame.

But let's hope the quantity left still holds some weight, because that filipendulous sense of shame is the only security Nigerians have between them and total governmental irresponsibility.

Unless, of course, Nigerians decide to take matters into their own hands.

PART FIVE
POLITICS
The Imposition of Governance

Our Heroes Past

(From "*The Anthem*")
The labours of those gone past
Often makes a nice repast
For campaign speeches and fundraisings.
Nice and tasteful trimmings
To gild the crass lusting of our heroes present.
Yet we do not attempt to resent
The unashamed squander of nomenclature
(by the parties and government—executive, legislature)
In the hypocrisy of the moment.
"Labours?" That's the past treatment
By founding fathers against social sickness.
Tell me, what's today's diagnosis?
What's the past hero got to say?
A resurrected Wiwa standing by the way,
Nzeogwu in his bloodied uniform,
Awolowo and constitutional reform,
Let Anikulapo once more bring out his sax
There's plenty of scandal arriving on the fax!
We'll dance on the grave of Bola Ige

It's only proper, we're still killing in relay.
Hang on, what more is to be said?
Clamp them, damp them, good thing they're dead.
We'll only shoot them all if they came again
Let's ask the Professor, but he's born again!
It's difficult to be a critic in a democracy
When the elected are full of hypocrisy
And bow, and scrape, and worship the hero
But what's in their head?—a lot of zero.

30

THE NIGERIANS THEY DON'T GIVE A DAMN ABOUT

A Rejoinder to Reuben Abati

Note: *Sometime in August 2012, Reuben Abati, the spokesman for President Goodluck Jonathan, wielded his pen and wrote an article titled: "The Jonathan They Don't Know" in praise of his boss and in rebuke of Nigerians. Abati's article was not well received, but this rejoinder was.*

"THEY" IN THIS TITLE REFERS to all the defence men, the pen-brandishing king's men, the unrelenting, self-appointed applauders, the cosy and established, comfortable, myopic and collective fathers of corruption, the distant crowd of Presidential addicts, the any-government-in-power cinema crowd of Nigeria, who seem to be in competition among themselves to achieve the favours of President Goodluck Jonathan.

This army of sponsored and self-appointed sycophants is so diverse; many of them don't even know when or how they should defend the President and neither do they understand, or "give a damn" about, the views or complaints of Nigerians.

The clear danger to public affairs commentary is that we have a lot of intelligent people initiating stupid clichés and too many unintelligent persons wasting public funds occupying offices established to lend relevance to these thoughtless clichés. Hold on. I don't want to be misunderstood. I am not saying nobody should defend the Nigerian President. I've spent some time understanding that social maxim: *"He who pays the piper calls the tune"*. Public position comes with its own share of sycophancy and grovelling. But the defending, praise-singing "Special Advisers" and maledicent "Senior Special Assistants" of the Jonathan regime must be guided by facts.

Let us gather our well-rounded stones. I have spent all my life as a Nigerian. I have watched the leadership of this country since I was capable of understanding such things. I can write a whole book on the Occupy Nigeria movement, but you won't get to read that until much later. I am certain that some government people will not buy the book if it gets written. Well, your choice. What I can state, for now is, that President Jonathan and his praise singers grossly misunderstand Nigerians. They think Nigerians are unfair to them. They criticise Nigerians as "ignorant". They accuse everyday Nigerians as mischievous. And when Nigerians dare to protest, they simply attribute it to the work of the opposition parties. How unfair!

Nigerians say he is a clueless President. A paid employee in the service of the President says Nigerians are wrong. Between Nigerians and the employee, who then is clueless? Nobody is more committed to the Nigerian Project than Nigerians themselves.

In spite of unforeseen challenges, in spite of decades of brutal military rule, in spite of a bloody civil war, in spite of continuous government corruption, Nigerians have done their best to remain one and fend for themselves both in private and public enterprise. And this year alone, President Jonathan has done his utmost best to increase the burden of Nigerians with a fuel price increase and its attendant consequences. Ordinary Nigerians protested against this. Let it be known now that those parading themselves as "Special Advisers" to the President, and who claim that the President still has the support of Nigerians, represent only themselves and their selfish salaried interests.

They say President Jonathan is a clever, methodical and intelligent man, and yet he is very adept at wrong footing majority of Nigerians, confusing the issues and distracting us from the main agenda. They say he understands the complexity of Nigeria, but he uses it to his advantage— for example, by turning May 29 into an opportunity to raise unneeded dust over June 12. But that aside, Nigerians do not care about his acutely conscious sense of history nor his personal reflection as a representative of all common persons. Nigerians only care about the results of his government's policy-making processes. Nigerians are not interested in sentimental expressions about the children of all blue collar workers who never wore shoes or got a chance to eat three-square meals, and whose mothers and aunties could never be part of policy-making processes.

And yet they say he understands Nigerians.

When Nigerians deride Jonathan about not wearing shoes as a child, they mean that as a metaphor for the irony of the President's purported penurious past contrasted to his clearly comfortable present, and the urgent need to redress such social inequalities. But I have read a "Special Adviser" responding literally that Nigerians meant that people should never vote for a man who never wore shoes. How simplistic! Attention needs to be drawn to the fact that a party-sourced President who has given no indication of how to transform Nigeria, and yet who campaigned on a platform of transformation, will always definitely be defended by those who consider themselves the children of the new regime, those who think that their descendants will inherit Nigeria. Wrong.

The Ijaws, the fourth largest ethnic nationality in Nigeria, have as much right to have their son as President as do the Nupe, the Tiv, the Efiks, the Ibibio and so many others—and nobody expects Jonathan to dwell on this. He may never have uttered an ethnic statement and he is not expected to do so. Must Nigerians applaud him for this? He is expected to see himself as the President of all Nigerians, which is why he lives in Aso Rock and not Bayelsa. He is expected to be at home with every group which is why he should listen to writings such as this.

They say he is focused on the challenges of nation-building but what about reinstating the President of the Court of Appeal? They say he wants to transform Nigeria, but this is based on an agenda only he knows about. They say he wants to unite the country yet he is creating avenues for popular protests, strikes and demonstrations. They say Nigerians want regular power supply and that he is working at it—but Nigerians don't want to cross 4, 400 MW on paper, they want to see it everywhere with their eyes.

Nigerians want infrastructure not a President who knows they want it. Nigerians want the Lagos-Ibadan Expressway fixed not an empty threat to the contractors. Nigerians want the East-West road fixed quickly not a mysterious directive to a particular nameless minister. Nigerians want to see corrupt people in jail, not just ineffective directives to government agencies. Nigeria's have no issue with foreign relations—they want charity to begin at home. They say he is transforming the agriculture sector, yet Nigerians still suffer expensive food items. The reason Nigerians do not go into a song and dance routine for President Jonathan is because they know that true rebranding of a nation is the actualisation of positive things—things that are already happening and not just a projection.

They say he is not "tribalistic". True. But how many Ijaws voted for President Jonathan compared to the rest of the country? Very few, I can tell you. Jonathan was voted in by Nigerians. Well, there are of course, all kinds of persons, special advisers and the like, who go about telling people that they have the President's ears and eyes. I have since learnt that some Nigerians consider it fashionable to wear the false garments created by public office.

They say the Presidency *qua* Presidency is staffed by key officials from all parts of the country, but are these officials efficient? They say the Secretary to the Government of the Federation is from Ebonyi State—but is he the best man for the job? They say the Chief of Staff and the Head of the President's Secretariat are both from Edo, but do they realise they have a wasteful budget? They say the Protocol Liaison Officer and Principal Private Secretary are from Adamawa, the Chief Detail is from Borno, the Aide De Camp (ADC) is from Kogi, the Perm Sec, State House is from Benue, the State Chief of Protocol is from Kwara, the Special Adviser, Media and Publicity is from Ogun, the Chief Physician to the President is from Rivers—but Nigerians want to know the criteria for their selection! They say only the Chief Security Officer, the Special Assistant, Domestic and the Special Adviser, Research and Strategy are from Bayelsa but Nigerians don't care about where they come from—Nigerians only care about what they have achieved!

They say when the President is in the office, he gets there early every day, and works till very late, and that he is exposed to all categories of Nigerians, but the same is true for even the market woman—especially the market woman. They say he runs a modern and open Presidency and yet he sends soldiers to the streets of Lagos. If he is on Facebook, Twitter, email, SMS, BB, and reads like they say, then he would realise that he has lost the approval of his initial support base—the people they call "idle and idling, twittering, collective children of anger, the distracted crowd of Facebook addicts, the BBM-pinging soap opera gossips of Nigeria". This is not even a provincial President—he is a cabal president. The purported intelligentsia in his immediate community should advise him to step out of office.

They say President Jonathan is the first Nigerian leader to appoint a woman as his Chief Economic Adviser as well as the Nigerian leader who opened up the Nigerian Defence Academy to women, but is this the meaning of progress? They say he took affirmative action in political appointments to a higher level by reserving 35 *per cent* of all appointive positions in government for the women folk, but is this why the First Lady must take a post as Permanent Secretary?

All these facts they point out may be incontrovertible but they are very irrelevant. Nigerians are not interested in whether a man occupies a position or whether a woman occupies it. Nigerians are not stupid! If it is a goat that will do the job well, Nigerians are happy to support the goat as a Minister! It will certainly not do any worse than the current ones are doing. They say the President's commitment to Nigeria is total, but what about his appointees? They say the President's children school in Nigeria, but do the children of his Ministers? Let the President wear any attire he enjoys, it is not his dress code that will promote Nigeria.

They say the President doesn't drink. Well, maybe he had better start drinking if that would make the administration more effective—what with all the choice drinks on every trip. What's the use of people who are not allowed to touch alcohol and yet have nothing to show for it? Alcohol is not served during official duties, but neither is it served at anyone's workplace either. Should we applaud the President for not drinking on the job? Even a student knows not to take alcohol in the classroom. Now they praise the President for not drinking alcohol and try to distort the issues at hand.

The budget states that the Presidential household intends to spend millions on feeding. Well, I have not enjoyed the privilege of eating at the President's table. But they say he eats fish pepper soup, Cassava Bread, slices of yam, rice, boiled plantain, fruits and vegetables. If this is the case, then why does the budget require millions of naira for his table? They say he fasts when he chooses, and fasts all month during Ramadan and Lent—this is all good, but we have our Bishops and Imams to do that for us. Nigerians do not care about his culinary habits or physical fitness regime. Let him drink *kainkain* if it will make him stronger, let him drink water if that would boost him. Let him fast if it will strengthen his arm, let him eat roasted turkey, and every delicacy under the sun if it would fire him up. Nigerians are not concerned whether the President is a glutton or not. Nigerians want a disciplined, hardworking president who has an effective plan for the country without burdening the people further.

Here is a man who started the 2012 New Year with indiscretion and insensitivity. As the proverb states: *The seeming hard worker who rushes to a task without applying common sense is, in fact, a lazy person trying to avoid being diligent.* The thing about the President's men is that they just cannot accept that Nigerians are intelligent enough to know what is right and what is wrong. This is the King George Complex. King George III of England could not accept the fact that the simple colonial Americans were sophisticated enough to decide how they wanted to be governed. And just like the colonial Americans gave chase to King George and his army of redcoats, Nigerians will eventually throw away these yes-men and promote a nation with men of integrity at the helm.

Let me end by saying that Nigerians, especially the "idle and idling, twittering, collective children of anger, the distracted crowd of Facebook addicts, the BBM-pinging" Nigerians, may be a simple people but simplicity is not naivety. If simplicity were to be naivety then the world would not be where it is today. It is simple people who gave shape to the likes of Abraham Lincoln, Mahatma Gandhi, Martin Luther King, and Kwame Nkrumah, simple people gave a mission to men who listened to the voice of the people—even when the special advisers around them were cajoling otherwise.

Random Flashes:
ON CIRCUMSTANCES
AND PRINCIPLES

Take a look at one of the daily instances that shows how people can be one thing somewhere and the opposite elsewhere. The bossy team leader becomes subservient when reporting to the MD, the usually irate MD becomes a snivelling lackey when discussing with the Chairman, the ordinarily arrogant Chairman toadies up to the Minister of Commerce, and the disciplinarian Minister is a "yes man" to the President. A man is confident in one place and a sycophant in another. A man is all for the truth in one place, carefully editorial in another.

Of course, philosophies change, and people abandon some principles and take up new ones. Russia moved away from the communist mindset and America is gradually moving away from absolute capitalism. But a change in principle should be more like the change of a caterpillar into a butterfly—which is fundamental, and not like the "change" of the chameleon—which is circumstantial. When reality proves a principle to be wrong and unworkable, by all means abandon it and fashion out a better one. As Lowell, said, the foolish and the dead alone never change their opinions.

And that's the bone of the matter: developing the ability to decipher between what is principled and what is circumstantial. Circumstances will always change. Life has always been cyclical. Your philosophies shouldn't be defined by who you are with, what position you occupy or where you are. Your principles should be identifiable and persistent. Because, at the end of the day, what we will remember are not the circumstances that surrounded you, but the person that you were.

31

THE RELUCTANT CANDIDATE
An Anti-Campaign Speech For Jonathan

Note: *I started out as one of the ardent supporters of Goodluck Jonathan's presidential bid in 2011, until I realised that the support wasn't required or valued. Having seen my error, and in penance for my misguided pro-GEJ campaigns of the time, I wrote an anti-campaign case on his behalf just prior to the 2011 elections.*

PERMIT ME A FEW MINUTES

GOODLUCK JONATHAN DOES NOT WANT to be Nigeria's next President. In fact, he did not aspire to become its current President. Instead, he has been pushed and shoved, pleaded with and threatened, harried and harassed into holding and contesting for a seat in one katzenjammer whirl of a circus show. However, in the midst of all this, Jonathan, silently and subtly has been trying to communicate that he doesn't want to be the president!

WHOM THE CAP DOESN'T FIT

Good luck shined on Jonathan when he was nominated as Vice President in 2007, but that was as far as the Bayelsan Governor aspired. After a stint of 8 years as Mr.Yar'Adua's vice, GEJ's hope was to retire to his village and live the life of a contented elder statesman. Sadly, on November 23, 2009, Mr. Umaru Yar'Adua, the silent President, took a one way trip to Saudi Arabia and scattered Jo's plans. But hang on a second, Yar'Adua did not die ASAP as any decent person should. Instead, he lingered on somewhat, disappeared, then gave a radio interview, and disappeared again, then showed up in the middle of the night in a coma, then disappeared, and then he died.

Now in the middle of this suspense-filled hide-and-seek game, a court hurriedly conferred Jonathan with powers to act on the President's behalf. This was on January 13, 2010. What should any right-thinking African Vice President do? If you say: declare a feast, have a thanksgiving service and start living the lavish life of a *de-facto* President, you'll be right. But not Jonathan, he kept on a bewildering act of "my boss is alive and well and probably working in the office next door" whereas the poor man lay in a coma on a Middle East hospital bed. Courts like to be obeyed, so the Supreme Court, in effect, gave him a phone call on January 22 and said, "Look man, get your act right and shape up—we give you 14 days". Or we'll kick your ass, they might have added.

Human nature abhors a vacuum, especially when it comes to political power, and people would rather have a reluctant president than no president. So, before the Supreme Court could kick Jonathan to jail, the legislature tried to save GEJ from himself and on February 9, 2010, passed a motion virtually locking Jonathan into the President's seat. This was greeted with mixed reactions by the cabinet members. But the louder the voice of the nay-sayers, the more popular Jo became. He became so popular, he was able to silence the nay-sayers. So he sacked the Attorney General, the number one nay-sayer.

Suddenly, on February 24, just as GEJ as president was beginning to look okay to we the people, Yar'Adua's lifeless body was rushed into Aso Rock by Turai and some armed forces dudes. Obviously, they planned to take the phrase "puppet president" very literally. This seemed a god-sent opportunity for Jonathan to resign, and he went into hiding without fuss. Unfortunately for both GEJ and Turai, the enchantments and prayers of the blessed imams, bishops and witchdoctors could not resurrect Yar'Adua into a zombie president. On May 5, Turai admitted defeat and called off the hide-and-seek game.

On May 6, Jonathan was sworn as president under duress. On May 7, Jonathan started goofing.

THE ART OF DOUBLESPEAK

GEJ has refined the art of doublespeak to new levels. Just as animals adapt to their surroundings for survival, GEJ has picked up doubletalk to protect himself from those who force him to hold power.

"Mr Jonathan, are you running for President?", "Well, not really, it's too early to decide, but I would bow to the wishes of the people". Can you make sense of that? I cannot either. I thought it was uncertainty until I realised it was a hidden cry for help. This man doesn't want to be president! In a country where Buhari was declaring his intention before the current term had even started, and IBB could declare with a tarnished record, and Atiku could announce his intention, even without a political party!

The trend continued with Jonathan rushing around to deny his statements or undo his actions. Jonathan said, Jonathan did not say. Jonathan did, Jonathan did not do, a continuous dance reminiscent of Yar'Adua's "now-you-see-me-now-you-don't" game, complete with drums. Jonathan has "yes" and "no" on several things: banning Nigerian soccer, denying Wikileaks, voting four times in 2007, militants bombing Abuja, everything, anything. Jo fools around with us.

THE CONFUSING FORMULA
Jonathan was being manoeuvred, chess-like, by the Ota Farmer and several others against whom he had no will to protest, but good luck threw in a zoning formula obstacle in Jo's way. GEJ was smart, and he knew the best way to rile up the North and guarantee opposition was to deny the zoning formula in the PDP constitution. He denied zoning. Well, zoning or no zoning, Nigerians didn't care. However, northern leaders did: and a move began to unite the North and stop Jonathan in his tracks. The strategy worked like a charm, that is, until the North goofed in a ridiculous way by selecting a blundering Atiku as its "consensus" candidate. A dead Jonathan would defeat an incumbent Atiku in a PDP primary. *You* would defeat Atiku in a PDP primary. Like a distressed scholar, Jonathan's plans to get a strong opponent from the north failed.

YOUTHFUL EXUBERANCE
How do you go about things if you want to ridicule a segment of society, grab its attention, dazzle it, and then spit in its face? Hence Jonathan's Facebook friendships. He wanted the youths to focus attention on him because he was planning to screw with them. In a big way. His hope was that the backlash would be just enough to guarantee he lost the votes of Nigerian youths. So what did he do? Once Jonathan was certain he had gathered enough attention

on Facebook and had even launched a book version of his chats (environmentalists, take note), he proceeded to insult the youths by appointing, unsolicited, two comedians as their politically-savvy representatives. Obviously, youthful employment cuts across a wide range of activity from advanced fee fraud to the medical profession: IT, journalism, legal practice, politics, the Civil Service, charity and NGOs, banks and financial institutions, audits and accounts, you name it . . . . But Jonathan desperately wanted to be disliked, so he picked a Big Brother Africa winner (this is not a joke) and a self-proclaimed entertainer as the wise leaders of all Nigerian youths—thereby lessening the academic motivations of all students nationwide. There is such a phrase as "going too far", even when you want to be disliked, but GEJ didn't give a damn. In fact, it soon became time for Jonathan to unleash his secret anti-president weapon—which brings us to the next point.

AN IMPATIENT WIFE

If there is one proof that Goodluck Jonathan intends to lose the coming election, then Patience it is. Her actions, independent as they seem, are definitely guided by her husband's instructions. She emerged from nowhere and, sentence by sentence, began to undo her husband's campaign. She antagonises governors and senators, alienates market women, workers, students, children and just about anybody who has had the chance to see her in action. The best point is this: she's so smart that her actions look convincing! But it's obvious to anyone with a thought to spare that one person can't be all that riotous! And yet, GEJ pretends to stand by, watching helplessly. "You know women," he says with a shrug to his advisers, "You just can't control them." Meanwhile, Patience loses him more votes in another state.

IN CONCLUSION

Goodluck Ebele Azikiwe Jonathan does not want your vote. He did not plan to be President. He does not want to be your president. He will do (or undo) anything to lose your vote. Do him a favour and please do not vote for him, there are more power hungry politicians out there who would appreciate your vote more. However, being the obstinate Nigerian that you are, you probably would vote for the unwilling candidate and bestow on a good man another 4 years of misery.

Random Flashes:
ON IMPEACHMENT

Here's how to impeach the President of the Federal Republic of Nigeria.

1.   *Prepare a detailed notice alleging that the President is guilty of gross misconduct in the performance of the functions of his office (let's call this the "Notice of Allegation").*

2.   *Have the Notice of Allegation signed by at least one-third of the National Assembly (i.e. at least, 157 persons) and have the signed document presented to the Senate President.*

3.   *Within 7 days of receiving the Notice of Allegation, the Senate President will send a copy of the Notice of Allegation to the President, and await a reply to the allegations in the document.*

4.   *Within 14 days of presenting the Notice of Allegation (and whether the President replies or not) each House*

of the National Assembly should pass a motion to investigate the allegations in the document.

5. The motion in number (4) above has to be passed by, at least, two-thirds of each House of the National Assembly, i.e. 240 Representatives, and 72 Senators.

6. If the motion is passed by each House of the National Assembly, the Senate President has to notify the Chief Justice of Nigeria to setup an investigative panel.

7. The investigative panel (the "Panel", for short) will consist of 7 persons appointed by the CJN. These folks must not be members of any public service, or any party or legislative house.

8. Of course, the President has a right to defend himself before the Panel either directly or through lawyers.

9. Within 3 months of commencing its investigations, the Panel has to report its findings to the National Assembly.

10. If the Panel reports that the allegations have not been proved, then that's the end of the matter.

11. *However, if the Panel reports that the allegations have been proved, then each House of the National Assembly will vote on whether to adopt the report.*

12. *Where two-thirds of each House of the National Assembly vote to adopt the report of the Panel, then the President stands removed from the date of the motion.*

Anybody who knows Nigerian politics and government well enough can see all the political loopholes in this process. Compare this with the US process, for example, and you can see why, to paraphrase Major Chukwuma Kaduna Nzeogwu's words, it is impossible to impeach a Nigerian President.

32

THAT CHIBOK MEETING

Note: *After much pressure from the local activists and the international community on the continuing mystery of the missing girls of Chibok, President Goodluck Jonathan finally agreed to meet with members of the community and the parents of the missing girls. Afterwards, Reuben Abati, the presidential spokesman, showed the world pictorial evidence of the belated meeting.*

NOW THAT THE PRESIDENT HAS met with the Chibok community, is he satisfied? Has his political paranoia been assuaged? Does he now believe the news of the abduction? Does the sad sight of despairing parents trigger some remorse for his late response? Has he drunk enough from the cup of their sorrow? Does he retract the negative statements made by his representatives in the last 100 days? Has the president learnt anything?

Probably not.

Probably, the president didn't have the meeting to learn anything from the community. Probably he didn't ask the parents what

AYO SOGUNRO

he could do to alleviate their pain. Most likely, he didn't commend the ordinary Nigerians who kept the Chibok tragedy fresh in the local and international news. In fact, if the press statements of the event, and the pictures released by Reuben Abati are any indication, the meeting was called by the president as an opportunity, as the Christian idiom says, to fulfil all righteousness.

Look at the pictures.

If you can take your admiring gaze away from the starchy shine of the president's attire, you will note that this was an unusual photo session. The faces in the pictures are a stark difference from the happy crowd and enthusiastic handshakes that characterise typical scenarios of presidential interaction.

Just look at the pictures.

The audience is sombre, still in shock. Some manage to look hopeful as they face the president; after all, they have been told, this is the man who can change everything for them. In one picture some women are crying. In another, a girl covers her face, presumably teary over the fate of her colleagues—or maybe just embarrassed at the shameful nature of the ceremony in which she was an involuntary participant.

For *this event is a shameful one, whether or not we acknowledge the indecency* of victims of a national tragedy being *permitted* to meet their ostensibly democratic leader. These are grieving men and women—and children too—and they have been compelled, despite their mood, to dress in their best and go see the president. And pictures are taken of them as they march past to see the leader. Not sympathetic pictures by bystanders—but professional photos taken by a paid staff.

And then these pictures are uploaded to the internet and tweeted to the world by a journalist-turned-hatchet man.

Pictures of a grieving people.

But hope is a powerful thing. And so the community went to Abuja with hope: never mind the insane display that has been made of their tragedy; never mind that Abuja is not Chibok; never mind the overwhelming opulence they are confronted with; never mind the soldiers, cameras and powerful officials that surround them; never mind their discomfort. Yes, they managed to dress fine, act sane and pose for the cameras. They stand still and act sane—in the hope that some definite and positive action would be taken to return their missing girls.

It takes a hard-hearted photographer to take these pictures without a lump in the throat. It takes a cynical journalist-turned-adviser to post these pictures and not hang himself afterwards. It takes a disbelieving president to meet with these parents and not lose composure. And why would the president lose composure? After all, his handlers chalk all policy criticism to opposition politics or mere disgruntlement, and so, they also have come to regard all policy decisions as an opportunity for counter politics, forgetting that humans—Nigerians—are affected by the outcome of their bloody games.

For no, *we still have no guarantee that the president is convinced of the seriousness of the situation.* A meeting is not an achievement; especially as the Presidency believes that, when it comes to *Boko Haram,* the evidence of presence is not the presence of evidence.

If Jonathan believes the truth of the abduction, he would immediately apologise to the parents and to Nigerians for the reactive tardiness, strip down to his work clothes, and preside over a 24-hour situation room to rescue the girls.

Instead, the president gave a lecture and the usual promises. Like royalty addressing the commoners, he *graciously* interacted with the community in the splendour of Abuja. And he took pictures with them over a red carpet.

Red carpet for a grieving community.

"Meet with the Chibok folks, you say? Well, we have met them. Now, smile for the cameras, everybody. Stand here, you stand there. Everyone say cheese!"

And so it is easy to conclude: the president isn't that much concerned with the missing girls. The president is more interested in being *seen* to be gracious. This meeting was not a sympathetic gesture by the Presidency—this meeting was, as admitted by the Presidency, at the instance of Malala, and its outcome is a promissory speech and a photo-op session.

Meeting over.

To these members of the Presidency, the people of Chibok are not humans to be dignified, but votes to be counted and PR opportunities to be exploited. *First they were dismissed as charlatans, next they were displayed as supplicants.* These parents had to be seen to be believed.

"Blessed are those who have not seen and yet believed" the biblical Jesus told a hard-nosed Thomas. But we can forgive the quest for empirical evidence by the president, we can forgive his public relations exploitation, we can forgive his aspersions on the activists who kept vigil for the girls—all is forgivable if a positive result is achieved.

But when will a positive result be achieved? For how many more days will this community continue to wait for its girls? No answers.

And so the president has seen the community, and Reuben Abati has tweeted the pictures. Is the president satisfied? Has his political paranoia been assuaged? Does he now believe the news of the abduction? Does the sad sight of despairing parents trigger some remorse for his late response? Has he drunk enough from the cup of their sorrow? Does he retract the negative statements made by his representatives in the last 100 days?

Has the president learnt anything?